Science Wisdom

科学から学ぶ知恵

Takayuki Ishii

Munekatsu Kajiyama

Joe Ciunci

photographs by
©iStockphoto.com
Getty Images
REUTERS/AFLO

音声ファイルのダウンロード/ストリーミング

CD マーク表示がある箇所は、音声を弊社 HP より無料でダウンロード/ストリーミングすることができます。トップページのバナーをクリックし、書籍検索してください。書籍詳細ページに音声ダウンロードアイコンがございますのでそちらから自習用音声としてご活用ください。

https://www.seibido.co.jp

Science Wisdom
科学から学ぶ知恵

Copyright © 2015 by Takayuki Ishii, Munekatsu Kajiyama, Joe Ciunci

*All rights reserved for Japan.
No part of this book may be reproduced in any form
without permission from Seibido Co., Ltd.*

はじめに

　情報化とグローバル化が進み、生活水準も高くなり、何でも便利になっている現代において、その社会を成立させている科学や技術のことを学ぶことは意義のあることです。その学びの中で、面白く奥深い側面を発見するものです。例えば、新幹線の技術にカワセミのくちばしの機能が応用されています。

　また、健康問題や環境問題など日々の生活に直接関係のあることにも、掘り下げると興味深いものが多くあります。生物にとって睡眠は大切なのですが、キリンは1日に20分ほどしか睡眠を取りません。これはなぜかを考えてみることも意義があることでしょう。

　本書は、科学的な面白話を、健康、環境、生物、技術、宇宙の5つの分野から4つずつ厳選して英語で学習する、「科学をテーマとした総合英語テキスト」です。

　各章に、そのトピックに関する語彙、内容把握、文法、作文、リスニングの問題を配置し、文法、表現、科学の雑学の3つのコラムがあります。

　本書は、語彙チェック、英文パッセージの原案、Notes、内容把握、文法および文法コラムを梶山が、作文、リスニング、表現と科学雑学のコラム、そして全体の監修を石井が、英文パッセージの執筆および練習問題をはじめとした全体の校閲をCiunciが担当しました。

　最後になりましたが、本テキストの出版に際し、成美堂編集部の菅野英一氏には大変お世話になりました。この場をお借りし、心より感謝申し上げます。

　本書が、科学分野における興味深い知識を身に付けつつ、英語の総合能力を高めることに貢献すれば、著者として、これ以上の歓びはありません。

著者代表
石井隆之

本書の使い方

■本書の構成
各章 5 ページで 20 章から成っています。

■本書のページ構成
<1ページ目～2ページ目>

Vocabulary Check	英文パッセージに現れる重要単語を5つ厳選し、その定義を選ぶ問題。
Passage	350~400 語程度の英文パッセージ。
Notes	重要な専門語や固有名詞、比較的レベルの高い単語・熟語などに関する注。
Comprehension	パッセージの内容理解をチェックする問題 5 問、正しい場合は T、間違いの場合は F を記入する。

<3ページ目>

Grammar	設定された文法テーマに関する文法問題 5 問。4 択式。
文法を理解する	文法の理解を深めるためのコラム。

<4ページ目>

Composition	丸かっこ内の単語の並べ換え問題 5 問。並べ換えるべき単語数は、各部を進むごとに増える。

    第 1 章～第 4 章   4つ
    第 5 章～第 8 章   5つ
    第 9 章～第 12 章 6つ
    第 13 章～第 16 章 7つ
    第 17 章～第 20 章 8つ

英語表現の小箱	英語表現の注意点に関するコラム。

<5ページ目>

Listening and Dictation	会話を聞いて、その空所に当てはまる単語を入れる問題。10 カ所に単語を入れる。
科学よもやま話	科学に関する面白雑学のコラム。

■本書の5大特長
その1 科学に関する興味深い情報を、英語で分かりやすく解説している。
その2 科学の分野を幅広く設定しているため、色々な分野のことが学べる。
その3 総合的に英語 4 技能を高めるために、さまざまな練習問題が入っている。
その4 練習問題にテーマを設定し、さらに章を追うごとにレベルを高めている。
その5 コラムが充実し、英文法と英語表現、そして面白情報を提供している。

目　次

第1部　健康　Health

Chapter 1　Animals' Sleeping Hours 1
　　　　　　　<キリンの睡眠は1日20分>

Chapter 2　The Mechanism of Hiccups 6
　　　　　　　<68年間しゃっくりが止まらなかった男>

Chapter 3　The Taste of Tears 11
　　　　　　　<うれし涙と悔し涙の味は異なる！>

Chapter 4　Male Brains and Female Brains 16
　　　　　　　<男は話が聞けず、女は地図が読めない？>

第2部　環境　Environment

Chapter 5　Light from Fireflies 21
　　　　　　　<西日本のホタルは2秒に1回、東日本のホタルは4秒に1回光る>

Chapter 6　Merits and Demerits of Pyramids 26
　　　　　　　<ピラミッド建設と森林破壊との関係>

Chapter 7　The Birth of the Hawaiian Islands 31
　　　　　　　<ハワイ諸島——南東の島ほど新しい理由>

Chapter 8　Bees and the Extinction of Man 36
　　　　　　　<ミツバチがいなくなると4年後に人類は絶滅する？>

第3部　生物　Organisms

Chapter 9　Herbivorous Horns 41
　　　　　　　<草食動物が角を生やす理由のいろいろ>

Chapter 10　Sunflowers and the Sun!? 46
　　　　　　　<ヒマワリが太陽の方を向く本当の原因>

Chapter 11　Trees of Greatness and the Greatness of Trees 51
　　　　　　　<世界の5つの偉大な樹木の話>

Chapter 12　Living Fossils 56
　　　　　　　<生きた化石の5つの条件>

第4部　技術　Technology

Chapter 13　*Electric Cars VS Hydrogen Cars* *61*
　　　　　　＜理想の車は孫悟空のキント雲？＞

Chapter 14　*The Future of Smartphones* *66*
　　　　　　＜スマホはどこまで進化するのか？＞

Chapter 15　*Technology Learned from Animals* *71*
　　　　　　＜蚊の刺し方が痛くない注射針の開発に貢献＞

Chapter 16　*Rainfall by Laser* *76*
　　　　　　＜昔は宗教のパワーで雨乞い、今は科学の力で人工降雨＞

第5部　宇宙　Universe

Chapter 17　*The Mystery of the Moon* *81*
　　　　　　＜月に地球2000年分のエネルギー源が存在？＞

Chapter 18　*Developments in Space Food* *86*
　　　　　　＜ラーメンや羊羹も宇宙食になる時代＞

Chapter 19　*Pluto* *91*
　　　　　　＜準惑星で134,340番目の小惑星になった冥王星＞

Chapter 20　*Is the Earth an Iron Planet?* *96*
　　　　　　＜地球は水の惑星というよりも鉄の惑星？＞

v

CHAPTER 1

Animals' Sleeping Hours

地球には身体の大きな生物や小さな生物、海で暮らす生物や陸で暮らす生物など、さまざまな生物がいます。では具体的に、睡眠時間が長い生物と短い生物は何でしょうか。また、それらの生物はどのくらいの時間眠るのでしょうか。

◀ VOCABULARY CHECK ▶

次の単語について、その定義を選び結びつけましょう。

1. rest・　　　・(A) to need something for a particular purpose
2. inhabit・　 ・(B) to live in a particular place
3. hang・　　 ・(C) to attach something to a hook or pole
4. digest・　　・(D) to break down foods in the stomach and intestines
5. require・　 ・(E) to relax, sleep or do nothing after a period of activity

PASSAGE

In a certain survey regarding humans' sleeping hours, the world averages 7 hours of sleep per day, though this differs more or less from country to country. Historically, Napoleon Bonaparte is believed to have slept only about three hours a day. His sleeping hours were quite short, but in the animal kingdom, there are some animals whose sleeping hours are a lot shorter than his. Among noteworthy animals in this field is the giraffe.

The giraffe, which is famous for its long neck, is also known to sleep very little, only about 20 minutes a day. Moreover, it usually sleeps while standing. Furthermore, it is said that it only needs one or two minutes of sleep to fully rest its brain. As for the reasons why it sleeps for such a short time, the following two are often mentioned:

In the first place, its short sleeping time is a result of the fact that it needs a larger amount of energy to support its body mass. Because giraffes eat food that is low in calories, they need to spend more time eating and less time sleeping.

The other reason it sleeps for a very short time a day is that it has to be careful not to be eaten by a carnivorous animal like a lion. To the lion, the giraffe is a great source of food because of its size.

On the other hand, there are some animals that sleep for a long time, in contrast with the giraffe. Many people may naturally think of sloths. They inhabit tropical forests in Central and South America, and spend almost their whole life hanging from a tree. Sleeping is no exception, as they even sleep while dangling from a tree.

It is true that they sleep about 20 hours a day, which is actually quite impressive, but there is an animal which sleeps even longer than the sloth: the koala, a herbivorous marsupial native to Australia.

The koala's sleeping hours are said to be about 22 hours a day. The reason for this extreme amount of sleeping time is related to its food. It mainly eats eucalyptus leaves, a toxic plant that takes a long time to digest. Moreover, as the leaves do not contain sufficient nutrition, the koala requires more sleep in order to conserve energy.

NOTES

average 平均とする / **kingdom** 界 / **noteworthy** 特筆すべき / **giraffe** キリン / **carnivorous** 肉食性の / **sloth** ナマケモノ / **tropical forest** 熱帯林 / **exception** 例外 / **dangle** ぶら下がる / **herbivorous** 草食性の / **marsupial** 有袋動物(胎盤がなく子宮内で子を育てられないので、未熟な状態で生まれた子供を下腹部にある袋の中で育てるという生態が特徴) / **eucalyptus** ユーカリ(主にオーストラリア原産の常緑高木で、その葉がコアラの餌になる) / **toxic** 有害な

COMPREHENSION

次の英文が本文の内容と一致する場合はT、一致しない場合はFを記入しましょう。

1. (　) Humans average about seven hours of sleep a day.
2. (　) A giraffe sleeps around three hours per day.
3. (　) Giraffes will not sleep much in order to protect themselves from carnivores.
4. (　) There are no animals that sleep more than sloths.
5. (　) The reason why koalas sleep so much lies in their food.

GRAMMAR

次の英文の空所に入れるのに正しい語句を (A) ～ (D) から選びましょう。

1. Because there is insufficient information about the job, please provide me with the most important requirement I (　　　) by e-mail.
   (A) needs　　(B) need　　(C) needing　　(D) need to

2. The diplomatic expert (　　　) a recent political incident during the televised debate.
   (A) mentioned
   (B) mentioned about
   (C) was mentioned
   (D) has mentioned about

3. The public (　　　) a bill to end high-handed methods of the ruling parties in the Diet.
   (A) is supported
   (B) is supporting
   (C) is supporting for
   (D) has supported for

4. Do you know of any foods (　　　) a high amount of antioxidants?
   (A) contain　　(B) contained of　　(C) containing　　(D) is containing of

5. We cannot turn back time, so it is very important to protect and (　　　) cultural heritage throughout the world.
   (A) conserve　　(B) conserve for　　(C) conserving　　(D) conserved for

---

＜文法を理解する＞　1. 自動詞と間違えやすい他動詞

次の問題を考えてみましょう。

　　You must (　　　) the matter.

　　(A) discuss　　(B) discuss about

これはTOEICなどでも頻出の項目です。選択肢のdiscussは「～について議論する」という意味なのでdiscuss aboutとしてしまいがちですが、discussは他動詞なので前置詞のaboutは不要となり、(A)が正解となります。このように自動詞と間違えやすい他動詞には、本問で扱った他に、次のようなものがあります。

accompany A（Aと一緒に行く）/ answer A（Aに答える）/ attend A（Aに出席する）/ enter A（A [建物など] に入る）/ inhabit A（Aに住む）/ marry A（Aと結婚する）/ oppose A（Aに反対する）/ reach A（Aに着く）/ resemble A（Aに似ている）

COMPOSITION

次の英文の(　　)内の単語を並べ換えて、意味の通る文にしましょう。

1. The amount of sleep needed (from / may / differ / animal) to animal.
   (　may differ from animal　)

2. The cheetah is (ability / its / for / famous) to run at extremely high speeds.
   (　famous for its ability　)

3. A plant-eating animal has to be (be / not / careful / to) eaten by a meat-eating animal.
   (　careful not to be　)

4. Onions are said to (Central / native / be / to) Asia.
   (　be native to Central　)

5. It is better for a teacher to always try to give his or her students the information (they / what / to / related) want to learn.
   (　related to what they　)

★英語表現の小箱1★　firstと前置詞を用いた表現

本文でin the first place（はじめに）が出てきましたが、他にfirstと前置詞を用いた重要表現を挙げておきます。

at first　はじめは
→ At first I thought English was difficult to learn.
（はじめは、英語を学ぶのは難しいと思っていました）

for the first time　はじめて
→ I saw kangaroos in the wild when I went to Australia for the first time.
（私がはじめてオーストラリアに行った時、野生のカンガルーを見ました）

from the first　はじめから
→ The man is a blabbermouth; therefore, I distrusted him from the start.
（あの男は口が軽い。だからはじめから信用しなかった）

Chapter 1 – *Animals' Sleeping Hours*

🎧 LISTENING & DICTATION   CD 1-3

次の会話を聞いて、空所に単語を埋めましょう。

A: I (1.   ) to oversleep. I average about (2.   ) hours of sleep a night.

B: What time do you usually go to bed?

A: At 2 a.m., since I (3.   ) in the afternoon. I usually (4.   ) up at around 10 a.m.

B: If you sleep (5.   ), you can live longer, I hear.

A: What is the (6.   ) number of sleeping hours in a day? I've heard that Japanese sleep fewer hours than other people in the world. Simply (7.   ), they are short sleepers.

B: You (8.   ) to sleep seven hours a day. According to a certain survey, those who sleep eight hours have a 20% higher (9.   ) of dying earlier than those sleeping seven hours.

A: And it's better to be asleep between 10 p.m. and 2 a.m., I hear.

B: It's impossible for me to go to bed at 10 p.m., but I try to go to sleep as (10.   ) as I can.

TIPS 科学よもやま話1　「居眠り」は国際語

　オーストリアの文化人類学者ブリギッテ・シテーガ氏によれば、睡眠については3つの文化パターンがあります。
　1．夜だけ眠る「単相睡眠文化」
　2．昼寝が制度化された「二相睡眠文化」
　3．各個人が気ままにうたたねできる「仮眠文化」

　日本は、3番目の仮眠文化に属しているようです。確かに日本では、電車で眠っていた人が降車駅でさっと立って出て行ったり、会議で眠っていたと思った人が突如話し出すなどの不思議な現象があります。

　厚生労働省は睡眠不足の勤労世代に対し30分以内の昼寝を推奨しています。プログラム化された昼寝は健康管理に不可欠だと考えられているからです。

CHAPTER 2
The Mechanism of Hiccups

ふとした瞬間に喉の奥がヒックと鳴ることがあります。いわゆる、しゃっくりです。では、しゃっくりはなぜ起こるのでしょうか。また、しゃっくりを止めるにはどのような方法があるのでしょうか。

◀ VOCABULARY CHECK ▶

次の単語について、その定義を選び結びつけましょう。

1. last   •   • (A) to stop functioning or existing
2. cause   •   • (B) to make something happen
3. cease   •   • (C) to try or plan to achieve something
4. aim   •   • (D) to continue for a particular period of time
5. feed   •   • (E) to give food to a person or animal

PASSAGE   CD 1-4

　Charles Osborne, who was from the State of Iowa in the U.S., was famous for the fact that his hiccups lasted for about 68 years starting in 1922. Though his hiccups did not stop, he continued to live a normal life, marrying twice and having 8 children.

5　During the 68 years of this condition, it is estimated that he hiccupped more than 430 million times, which led to a GUINNESS world record.

　The real cause of hiccups is said to be twitches of the diaphragm. The particular sound of "hick" is caused by the closing of the vocal cords. Then why does the diaphragm go into convulsions in the first place? The cause for this 10　still remains unknown, but the spasms may occur when one quickly drinks something hot, ingests spices, violently laughs or coughs, and drinks alcohol in one gulp. Though rare, hiccups may also occur because of kidney trouble or brain tumors.

　Though in most cases, hiccups will not last long and will cease naturally.
15　Besides the rather dramatic method of frightening the hiccupping person

suddenly from behind, home remedies for stopping hiccups include the act of respiring with a paper bag to one's mouth as well as the act of drinking water, pulling one's tongue, or rubbing one's eyes. The former remedy aims at stopping hiccups by causing a higher concentration of carbon dioxide in the blood; the latter aims at stimulating the vagus nerve, one of the cranial nerves, to stop hiccups.

Moreover, the remedies of awkwardly drinking water from the opposite rim of a glass by bending forward or drinking a kind of tea made from the hull of a persimmon also are effective methods.

Babies are prone to hiccups due to their still developing diaphragms. If a diaper gets wet or they inhale too much air in one gulp when they drink breast milk or milk from a feeding bottle, hiccups may occur.

If you raise an infant's temperature by warming their body or feeding them milk, their hiccups may stop. Hiccupping babies usually look annoyed and uncomfortable, but this is a normal part of their development and nothing to worry about.

NOTES

hiccup しゃっくり / **twitch** 痙攣[けいれん] / **diaphragm** 横隔膜(呼吸運動に関与する筋肉の1つで、thoracic diaphragmとも表現) / **vocal cord** 声帯(vocal chordとも表現) / **go into ~** ～を起こす / **convulsion** 痙攣[けいれん] / **spasm** ひきつり / **ingest** 摂取する / **spice** 香辛料 / **in one gulp** 一気飲みで(drink ~ in one gulpで「～を一気に飲む」、down ~ in one gulpで「～を一息で飲み干す」という意味になる) / **kidney trouble** 腎臓病 / **brain tumor** 脳腫瘍 / **home remedy** 民間療法 / **respire** 呼吸する / **rub** こする / **concentration** 濃度 / **carbon dioxide** 二酸化炭素 / **vagus nerve** 迷走神経 / **cranial nerve** 脳神経 / **bend forward** 身をかがめる / **hull** へた / **persimmon** 柿 / **be prone to ~** ～しやすい / **diaper** おむつ / **inhale** 吸い込む / **breast milk** 母乳

COMPREHENSION

次の英文が本文の内容と一致する場合はT、一致しない場合はFを記入しましょう。

1. (　) Charles Osborne had over 430,000,000 hiccups.
2. (　) Hiccups are caused by convulsions of the diaphragm.
3. (　) All the home remedies for stopping hiccups aim at stimulating the vagus nerve.
4. (　) Infants never have hiccups.
5. (　) Babies' hiccups are not a problem, because they are part of their proper developmental process.

GRAMMAR

次の英文の空所に入れるのに正しい語句を(A)〜(D)から選びましょう。

1. Mr. Saito adores shopping. However, he must try to control his urges lest he (　　　) bankrupt.
   (A) go　　　　(B) goes　　　　(C) going　　　　(D) went

2. The country may have nuclear weapons, which (　　　) a destabilizing factor in this region.
   (A) remained　　(B) remains　　(C) remaining　　(D) was remained

3. It simply had never (　　　) me that the actress in this Asian film was Japanese.
   (A) occurred　　(B) occurred to　　(C) being occurred　　(D) occurring to

4. The burglary (　　　) during the short time when the shop owner was gone.
   (A) happened　　(B) happened to　　(C) happened it　　(D) happened that

5. You (　　　) a little bit pale. If you have a fever, you should see a doctor.
   (A) look　　(B) look at　　(C) are looked　　(D) having looked

＜文法を理解する＞　2. 他動詞と間違えやすい自動詞

次の問題を考えてみましょう。

　　I (　　　) my friend for telling a lie.
　　(A) apologized　　(B) apologized to

これはTOEICなどでも頻出の項目です。選択肢のapologizeは「謝る」という意味で、日本語で「〜を謝る」と言えるので他動詞としてしまいがちですが、apologizeは自動詞です。直後に人を表す名詞が来る場合、前置詞のtoが必要となるので、(B)が正解となります。このように他動詞と間違えやすい自動詞は他に次のようなものがあります。各自動詞が伴う前置詞を加えた形で示しています。
agree with A（[気候などが] Aに合う、Aと意見が一致する）/ complain to A about B（BのことでAに不平を言う）/ arrive at[in] A（Aに到着する）/ get to A（Aに到着する）/ attend on A（Aに仕える）/ attend to A（Aに注意する）/ enter into A（A [議論など] を始める / graduate from A（Aを卒業する）/ marvel at A（Aに驚く）/ consent to A（Aに同意する）/ object to A（Aに反対する）/ participate in A（Aに参加する）/ reply to A（Aに答える）/ hope for A（Aを望む）

COMPOSITION

次の英文の(　　)内の単語を並べ換えて、意味の通る文にしましょう。

1. Ms. White (State / was / the / from) of Nebraska, U.S.A.
   (　　　　　　　　　　　　　　　　　　　　　　　　　　　　　　　)

2. The necessity of being able to get in contact with people quickly (the / to / invention / led) of telephones.
   (　　　　　　　　　　　　　　　　　　　　　　　　　　　　　　　)

3. A stomachache may occur not (of / only / because / food) poisoning but due to too much mental stress.
   (　　　　　　　　　　　　　　　　　　　　　　　　　　　　　　　)

4. People will be surprised if you suddenly shout (behind / them / from / at), especially if you approach them quietly before doing so.
   (　　　　　　　　　　　　　　　　　　　　　　　　　　　　　　　)

5. Quantum mechanics usually (describing / at / aims / what) happens in the microscopic world, which cannot be explained by classical mechanics.
   (　　　　　　　　　　　　　　　　　　　　　　　　　　　　　　　)

★英語表現の小箱2★　＜the V-ing of O＞の構造

　本文でthe closing of the vocal cordsが出てきましたが、これはclosing the vocal cordsという動名詞句を、さらに言い換えたもので、一層名詞的になったといえます。一般に、V-ing O（＝OをVすること）は、the V-ing of Oと言い換えることができます。この構造は名詞性が強くなっているので、形容詞を---ingの直前に置くこともできます。また、副詞を後ろにつけることはできません。

例：　○ the reading of magazines
　　　○ the quick reading of magazines
　　　× quick reading magazines
　　　× the reading of magazines quickly
　　　○ reading magazines quickly

LISTENING & DICTATION

CD 1-5

次の会話を聞いて、空所に単語を埋めましょう。

A: I have been hiccupping (1.   ) this morning. I seem to have hiccups (2.   ) too often. Why is this happening all of a sudden?

B: It is said that this condition is (3.   ) by convulsions of the diaphragm.

A: Why does that (4.   )? What causes the convulsions?

B: At this point it is not (5.   ). But there are many remedies for hiccups. Among them, the most effective way is to (6.   ) one's breath.

A: Can you be a little more (7.   )?

B: OK. Just stand up, and take a deep breath. Then stop breathing for about 30 seconds. During that time, it is important to (8.   ) your abdominal muscles. And that's all. Simple, right?

A: I'll give it a try. ・・・Oh, my hiccups seem to have stopped. This is great. And simple, too!

B: Well, taking deep breaths is an (9.   ) part of maintaining good health. Just be careful (10.   ) to hold your breath for too long!

TIPS 科学よもやま話２　世界のしゃっくりの止め方

世界にはユニークなしゃっくりの止め方があります。一部を紹介しましょう。

1. アメリカ　**２５セントコイン法**
   しゃっくりで困っている人に２５セントをあげます。驚いて、しゃっくりが止まります。

2. ベトナム　**質問攻め法**
   しゃっくりをしている子供にいろいろ質問しているうちに、自然に止まります。

3. カンボジア、モンゴル　**盗みの嫌疑法**
   子供の場合、盗みを疑って子供を責めると、子どもは悲しみ、しゃっくりは止まります。

4. イスラエル、スロベニア　**砂糖水飲み法**
   グラスの中の水に砂糖をスプーン２杯入れてかき混ぜ、一気にがぶ飲みします。

5. メキシコ　**眉間に赤紙貼り付け法**
   眉間に赤い紙や赤いテープを貼ると、しゃっくりは止まります。

CHAPTER 3

The Taste of Tears

ヒトは甘い・辛いといった味を感じたり、さまざまな時に涙を流したりする生き物です。ヒトが味を感じたり涙を流したりするメカニズムはどのようなものなのでしょうか。また、涙にも味があるらしいのですが…。

◀ VOCABULARY CHECK ▶

次の単語について、その定義を選び結びつけましょう。

1. taste・   ・(A) a feeling of great sadness
2. tongue・   ・(B) pressure or worry caused by the problems
3. stress・   ・(C) the muscular structure that moves and tastes food
4. sorrow・   ・(D) the feeling produced by a particular food or drink
5. anger・   ・(E) a strong feeling that is often connected to violence

PASSAGE

"Keep in mind that there is a profound world of taste out there that everyone should experience." —This phrase was uttered by the artist Kitaoji Rosanjin, who was also famous as a gourmet. The way we taste things, from food to even our tears, is fascinating.

Taste cells inside the 5,000-odd taste buds on the surface of the human tongue are stimulated by objects such as food. They then send the information about the taste to the brain through the gustatory nerve, which finally allows us to perceive its taste.

Generally speaking, it had long been thought that different parts of the tongue could perceive different tastes. For example, sweetness is made manifest at the tip of the tongue. However, as of the present, this theory has been negated, replaced by another theory that even a single taste bud can process every taste.

Besides food, people are also capable of noticing distinct differences in the taste of tears. Tears are usually shed in the following two cases: for physical protection and while under emotional stress.

The former tears are a physiological response to protect eyes from foreign objects, smoke, and bacteria, and such, or to disinfect eyes from things like poisonous chemicals. When we cut an onion, we naturally shed tears. The tears will protect the eyes from the stimulus caused by the chemical agent emitted from the onion as it is sliced.

It is possible to prevent this problem. It is considered effective to use a kitchen knife that cuts well, to soak the onion in water first, or to cool it in the refrigerator before cutting. These all help remove the tear-inducing stimulus of onions.

The latter kinds of tears related to emotions are shed when we are agitated by external stressors, both positive and negative. However, different feelings cause different tastes of tears. Tears shed at the time of sorrow or joy are less salty because the concentration of sodium contained in them becomes low due to the predominance of the parasympathetic nerves. On the other hand, tears shed out of anger or shame taste more salty because of the high concentration of sodium due to the predominant sympathetic nerves.

The taste of tears is an interesting topic to us all, as it is something we all experience and can instantly identify with.

 NOTES

profound 奥深い / **Kitaoji Rosanjin** 北大路魯山人(1883-1959, 陶芸家) / **gourmet** 美食家 / **taste cell** 味細胞(味を感じる細胞) / **~-odd** ~余りの / **taste bud** 味覚芽, 味蕾[みらい](舌などにある食べ物の味を感じる小さな器官) / **gustatory nerve** 味覚神経 / **perceive** 知覚する / **as of ~** ~現在 / **negate** 否定する / **shed** (涙などを)流す / **physiological** 生理的な / **foreign object** 異物 / **~ and such** ~など(= and so on) / **disinfect** 消毒する / **poisonous** 有害な / **chemical** 化学物質(通例、複数形) / **chemical agent** 化学物質 / **emit** 放出 / **soak** 浸す / **tear-inducing** 涙を誘う / **stressor** ストレス因子(環境の変化の刺激に適応しようとした際に心身はさまざまな変化を起こすが、この変化をストレス反応と呼び、ストレス反応を起こす原因をストレス因子と呼ぶ) / **concentration** 濃度 / **sodium** ナトリウム / **predominance** 優勢 / **parasympathetic nerve** 副交感神経(自律神経の1つで、中脳・延髄・仙髄から出ている) / **predominant** 有力な / **sympathetic nerve** 交感神経(自律神経の1つで、脊髄から出ている)

COMPREHENSION

次の英文が本文の内容と一致する場合はT、一致しない場合はFを記入しましょう。

1. (　) The human brain senses the taste of foods.
2. (　) The theory that different parts of the tongue recognize different types of tastes is still well accepted at present.
3. (　) Humans shed tears only when influenced by external stressors.

4. (　) Tears shed of joy are watery and tasteless.
5. (　) Tears shed through sadness taste different from tears shed when one is happy.

GRAMMAR

次の英文の空所に入れるのに正しい語句を (A) 〜 (D) から選びましょう。

1. Our job has been (　　　) very easy to handle since our company's president introduced the new computer system.
   (A) make　　　(B) makes　　　(C) making　　　(D) made

2. During the height of the revolution, a lot of innocent people's blood was (　　　).
   (A) shed　　　(B) sheds　　　(C) shedded　　　(D) shedding

3. The company's reputation suffered greatly after a counterfeit check attributed to them (　　　).
   (A) circulates　(B) was circulated　(C) to circulate　(D) being circulated

4. In general, it has long (　　　) that men are naturally superior to women, but that is wrong.
   (A) thought　(B) thought of　(C) been thinking　(D) been thought

5. This book has (　　　) a classic virtually since the day of its publication. Actually, it has sold more than a million copies.
   (A) consider　(B) considered　(C) been considered　(D) been considering

＜文法を理解する＞　3. 受動態と前置詞 by

次の問題を考えてみましょう。
　　(1) Tom was (　　　) everyone.　　(2) Tom was (　　　) everyone.
　　(A) laughed at　(B) laughed at by　　(A) known to　(B) known by

　(1)の選択肢にある laugh at は群動詞と呼ばれるもので、laugh at という1つの塊が他動詞として機能しています。受動態の場合、能動態の主語を表す際には by が必要となるので、(B) が正解となります。laugh at A は「A を笑う」という意味です。
　一方で(2)の選択肢にある known to という表現は、能動態の主語である everyone が意志を持っていないので受動態では by 句を用いず、その代わりに to を用いたものです。(A) が正解となります。なお、be known to A (A に知られている) の他に、be known for A (A で知られている) / be known by A (A で分かる) [この by が行為者を示す by ではないので、A は能動態の主語でない] / be known as A (A として知られている) / be covered with A (A で覆われている) / be satisfied with A (A に満足している) / be caught in A (A [雨など] に遭う) などの表現が重要です。

✏ COMPOSITION

次の英文の（　　）内の単語を並べ換えて、意味の通る文にしましょう。

1. You should (mind / in / that / keep) it is important to sleep between 10 p.m. and 2 a.m.
   (　　　　　　　　　　　　　　　　　　　　　　　　　　　　　　　　)

2. Mt. Fuji, (the / of / present / as), is not a dormant volcano; it is an active volcano.
   (　　　　　　　　　　　　　　　　　　　　　　　　　　　　　　　　)

3. Some animals are able to change their skin color to blend with the color of their surrounding environment in order to (from / themselves / their / protect) natural enemy.
   (　　　　　　　　　　　　　　　　　　　　　　　　　　　　　　　　)

4. It (see / possible / to / is) third-magnitude stars, which number about 190, with the naked eye.
   (　　　　　　　　　　　　　　　　　　　　　　　　　　　　　　　　)

5. Generally speaking, many physicists explore the mysterious aspects of space and time (of / curiosity / out / simply).
   (　　　　　　　　　　　　　　　　　　　　　　　　　　　　　　　　)

★英語表現の小箱3★　＜自動詞＋副詞＞の注意すべき表現

本文でcut well（よく切れる）が出てきましたが、＜自動詞＋副詞＞の形には注意すべき表現があります。

　　He writes badly.（彼は字が下手だ）
　　He writes poorly.（彼は文章が下手だ）
　　This pen writes well.（このペンはよく書ける）
　　Her new book is selling well.（彼女の新しい本はよく売れている）
　　Her old book is selling badly.（彼女の古い本は売れ行きが悪い）

Chapter 3 – *The Taste of Tears*

🎧 LISTENING & DICTATION CD 1-7

次の会話を聞いて、空所に単語を埋めましょう。

A: You look (1.   ). Wait, are you crying? Want to talk about the (2.   ) why?

B: I just got back from my tennis tournament. I lost. I still can't believe it.

A: I (3.   ) your tears taste (4.   ), right? Did you know the taste of tears differs according to your feelings? Tears shed in anger or humiliation are salty.

B: Wait a sec…these don't (5.   ) that salty. A little, but nothing like sea water.

A: The concentration of salt in tears is about 0.5%; on the (6.   ) hand, that of sea water is about 3.5%. So, of course water from the sea is saltier.

B: Okay. Tears of (7.   ) are salty. Then what about tears of happiness?

A: They are not so salty. Tears shed when you are sad also have no taste.

B: Tears of (8.   ) and sadness are both tasteless? That's (9.   ) of strange since the feelings of happiness and sadness are completely different, so it makes more (10.   ) for the taste to be different, too.

TIPS 科学よもやま話3　涙は血液から出来ている！

　血液は何で出来ているのでしょう。水のような成分で血液の50〜60％を占め、栄養を運び老廃物を回収する「血漿（けっしょう）」、酸素を運ぶ「赤血球」、ばい菌を退治する「白血球」、そして、傷口をふさぐ「血小板」の主に4つから成っています。

　涙が出る腺を涙腺と呼びますが、この涙腺を通れないのが、赤血球と白血球、血小板の3つです。だから、涙は、血液とほぼ同じ成分ですが、赤血球と白血球、血小板が入っていないのです。

CHAPTER 4

Male Brains and Female Brains

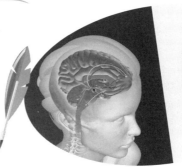
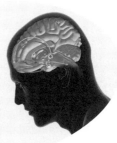

ヒトには男性と女性があり、両性にはさまざまな点で異なった特徴があります。そして、その違いに脳が関与している場合があります。男性と女性の脳の違いはどのような差異を生むのでしょうか。

◀ VOCABULARY CHECK ▶

次の単語について、その定義を選び結びつけましょう。

1. typical   ・   ・ (A) extremely large in size or amount
2. decisive ・   ・ (B) having the usual qualities or features
3. creative ・   ・ (C) not sensible or thought out in a logical way
4. huge   ・   ・ (D) vital for the final result of a particular situation
5. illogical ・   ・ (E) involving the use of skill to produce something new

PASSAGE

　The book entitled "Why Men Don't Listen and Women Can't Read Maps" sold 6.6 million copies across the world more than 10 years ago. This book attracted worldwide attention because it focused on the fact that men and women have different thinking patterns.

5　Differences in the way of thinking are attributed to differences in brain functions. Different brains are formed by different hormones. For example, the main male hormone, androgen, contributes to masculinity. The disparity in children's illustrations between infant boys and girls can also be traced back to the difference in brains. Among the typical examples showing variances in
10 brains is the fact that boys are more likely to draw pictures of planes or cars, while girls often draw flowers or cute animals.

　There are structural differences between male and female brains. The corpus callosum of the female brain is actually roundish and larger than that of males'. Therefore, many experts think the difference of this part of the brain
15 is a decisive factor when distinguishing between men and women in regard to

certain situations. For instance, women have good intuition because the exchange of information between the left brain engaging in logical and scientific thinking and the right brain focusing on creative and artistic feelings is quite smooth through their wide corpus callosum.

A huge amount of information may pass through the organ, creating the tendency of women to panic more often than men. If a drawing of a building design is shown, only a certain part of the male brain reacts, but in the case of females, cerebral activity shows signs of instability; therefore, women may have weaker space perception than men, leading to women being unable to read maps well.

Finally, men tend to talk logically using their left brain, while women use both the right and left halves due to the width of their corpus callosum. So, women are more naturally talkative with personal feelings or illogical remarks interjected into their conversation. Because men are more interested in the parts of the talk reflecting logic and reasoning, they are not always attentive listeners of females.

NOTES

entitle ～ ～にタイトルをつける / **hormone** ホルモン（特殊な生理作用がある生物の分泌物。ホルモンはギリシャ語で「刺激する」という意味のhormaeinを語源とする）/ **androgen** アンドロゲン（生体内で働くステロイドホルモンの1つで、男性ホルモンや雄性ホルモンとも呼ばれる）/ **masculinity** 男らしさ / **disparity** 相違（＝variance）/ **corpus callosum** 脳梁［のうりょう］（左右の大脳半球をつなぐ太い束のこと）/ **distinguish** 区別する（distinguish A and Bで「AとBを区別する」）/ **have good intuition** 勘がいい / **organ** 器官，臓器 / **drawing** 製図 / **building design** 建築設計 / **cerebral** 脳の / **instability** 不安定 / **space perception** 空間知覚 / **illogical remark** 不合理な発言 / **interject** 不意に差し挟む

COMPREHENSION

次の英文が本文の内容と一致する場合はT、一致しない場合はFを記入しましょう。

1. (　) Differences in ways of thinking may be attributed to the differing ways people's brains function.
2. (　) Androgen is a hormone which contributes to femininity.
3. (　) The corpus callosum of a male brain is smaller than that of a female brain.
4. (　) Women are not as good at spatial recognition compared to men.
5. (　) Men are likely to listen carefully to women's stories.

GRAMMAR

次の英文の空所に入れるのに正しい語句を (A) ～ (D) から選びましょう。

1. (　　　) of winter makes me feel like hopping on a plane and flying to a warm southern country.
   (A) Think　　　(B) Thinking　　　(C) Thought　　　(D) Thinkable

2. (　　　) me a Rembrandt painting at the museum, she proudly explained its painting techniques.
   (A) Show　　　(B) Showing　　　(C) Shown　　　(D) Showy

3. I strongly object to Mary (　　　) forced to work overtime even once a month, because of her delicate constitution.
   (A) having　　　(B) being　　　(C) been　　　(D) has

4. Ten computers (　　　) the new operating system are scheduled to be installed in our office.
   (A) use　　　(B) user　　　(C) using　　　(D) used

5. Bob was (　　　) that his neighbor was responsible for the crime, for which he was later arrested.
   (A) mention　　　(B) mentions　　　(C) mentioning　　　(D) mentioned

<文法を理解する>　4. –ing の用法

次の例文について考えてみましょう。

(1) I am <u>playing</u> soccer.（私はサッカーをしています）
(2) <u>Smoking</u> is not allowed here.（ここでは禁煙です）
(3) I saw the <u>running</u> dog.（私は走っている犬を見ました）
(4) I saw the dog <u>running</u>.（私は犬が走っているのを見ました）
(5) <u>Opening</u> the door, I found my mother was there.（ドアを開けた時、母がいました）

(1) ～ (5) の英文中の -ing は、(1) が進行形、(2) が動名詞、(3) が現在分詞（名詞修飾）、(4) が現在分詞（補語）、(5) が現在分詞（分詞構文）です。文法問題を解く場合はもちろん、英文を読んだり書いたりする場合にも、これらを識別できることが重要です。

Chapter 4 – *Male Brains and Female Brains*

COMPOSITION

次の英文の(　　)内の単語を並べ換えて、意味の通る文にしましょう。

1. Einstein (idea / on / focused / the) that the speed of light is fixed and unchangeable.
   (　　　　　　　　　　　　　　　　　　　　　　　　　　　　　　　　)

2. Differences in animals' life expectancy (to / can / attributed / be) their varying heart rates.
   (　　　　　　　　　　　　　　　　　　　　　　　　　　　　　　　　)

3. The biologist's interest in tortoises can (back / to / traced / be) her childhood, when she kept one as a pet.
   (　　　　　　　　　　　　　　　　　　　　　　　　　　　　　　　　)

4. The astronomer (the / in / engaged / was) study of the planet's unusual orbit around its star for years but still cannot explain the reason for it.
   (　　　　　　　　　　　　　　　　　　　　　　　　　　　　　　　　)

5. The degree to which people exhibit their scientific genius totally depends on whether they are interested (seen / details / in / normally) as trifling.
   (　　　　　　　　　　　　　　　　　　　　　　　　　　　　　　　　)

★英語表現の小箱4★　　集中と没頭の表現

本文でfocus on ～（～に焦点を当てる）やengage in ～（～に従事する）が出てきましたが、onやinは、動詞や形容詞に付くと、「集中や没頭」の意味を表すことが多いので注意しましょう。

　例：　center on ～（～を中心とする）
　　　　concentrate on ～（～に集中する）
　　　　be bent on ～（～に熱心である）
　　　　be keen on ～（～に熱中している）
　　　　be absorbed in ～（～に没頭している）
　　　　be lost in ～（～に没頭している）
　　　　be immersed in ～（～に没頭している）[=immerse oneself in ～]

LISTENING & DICTATION

次の会話を聞いて、空所に単語を埋めましょう。

A: I just (1.   ) the latest test and now I'm in danger of flunking out. I'm hopeless. I really didn't study (2.   ) enough. It's said that even Einstein used only 10% of his brain. I probably didn't (3.   ) use 1% of mine.

B: Even though that theory is popular, it's just not true. This idea probably spread because the nerve cells in the brain (4.   ) for about 10% of the cells of the whole brain. In fact, people are more likely to use their brains to their fullest (5.   ) when making an actual effort in something.

A: So, some "facts" we take for (6.   ) are not always true, huh? I didn't know that. By the way, how many nerve cells are there in the brain?

B: There are about 30 (7.   ) brain cells, which is the maximum, but this amount applies to our infancy, or so I hear.

A: I once heard that the number of cells starts to decrease after you reach the age of 20.

B: That's (8.   ). We often hear that 100,000 nerve cells are depleted every day after 20, but the fact seems to be that about 70% of them are gone by the age of two.

A: I see. Rumor and facts are worlds (9.   ). Anyway, I can use my entire brain. I'm relieved.

B: Your pathetic test score has nothing to do with your brain. It actually (10.   ) your lack of effort!

TIPS 科学よもやま話4　昆虫の脳の不思議

　地球上の全ての動物種の3分の2が昆虫といわれているので、地球は昆虫王国といえるでしょう。そんな昆虫にも脳があります。脳はもちろん頭部にありますが、人間の脊髄に似た神経繊維の束は、ヒトと異なり腹側にあります。

　昆虫を下等だと決めつけるわけにはいきません。巣を持つ昆虫のほとんどは、巣の周りの景色をしっかり覚えていることが実験で確認されています。

　また、ミツバチは蜜を取る目的の花の形、色、匂い、その場所や開花の時期などを学習により学びとり、他のハチにその方向と距離をダンスによって情報伝達しています。これも高度に発達した脳のおかげであるといえるでしょう。

　昆虫は、記憶・学習・情報伝達に優れているのです。それを脳がつかさどっているのですから、昆虫もなかなか隅に置けませんね。

CHAPTER 5

Light from Fireflies

光を発する生き物、ホタル。その中でも、有名なゲンジボタルとヘイケボタルは西日本と東日本で異なる特徴があるのですが、それは一体何なのでしょうか。また、それらのホタルの生息分布の境目は日本列島の生成と関連があるらしいのですが…。

◀ VOCABULARY CHECK ▶

次の単語について、その定義を選び結びつけましょう。

1. home
2. intensely
3. completely
4. gradually
5. representative

- (A) in every way possible
- (B) to or at the place where you live
- (C) by using or showing extreme force or degree
- (D) slowly, over a long period of time
- (E) typical of a particular group

PASSAGE

Earth is home to living creatures like sea-fireflies, firefly squids and luminous moss which have the ability to emit light. Among the most famous light-emitting animals are fireflies.

It is said that there are more than 40 species of fireflies in Japan. Among the most common species of fireflies are the Genji firefly and the Heike firefly.

One of the noteworthy things about these fireflies is that the male Genji firefly is known to display different traits in Western Japan and Eastern Japan. We can say that this is a kind of "dialect of light," in a sense.

First, there is a difference in the periodicity of emitted light. The male of the Genji firefly in Western Japan emits light once every two seconds, while that of the firefly in Eastern Japan does this once every four seconds.

Secondly, the difference is also confirmed in the peak time of luminescence. The male fireflies in Western Japan give off light most intensely at around 8:30 p.m., whereas those of Eastern Japan radiate light most strongly at about 7:45 p.m.

Where can we draw the border between Western and Eastern Japan in terms of Genji fireflies? The boundary line seems to correspond to the Fossa Magna, or the great central rift zone in Japan, which divides Eastern and Western Japan. This rift zone is known to have contributed to the division of species into new sets of species, a trend which continues. This could happen to the Genji fireflies too; it is still possible for them to develop into two completely different species, though at present this is only conjecture.

The life-altering Fossa Magna began forming during the early geographical stages of Japan. At the early stage of Japan's formation, there was a shallow sea between Southwestern Japan and Northeastern Japan, but at the time of crustal movements which occurred several million years ago, this sea gradually rose to form the Fossa Magna.

Dr. Nobuyoshi Ohba, Japan's representative authority on fireflies, used the recent development of genetic engineering to allow him to make a plant emit light by incorporating a luminescence-related gene extracted from a firefly into a plant in 1993.

NOTES

sea-firefly ウミホタル(体長が3ミリ程度の甲殻類) / **firefly squid** ホタルイカ / **luminous moss** ヒカリゴケ / **the Genji firefly** ゲンジボタル(Luciola cruciataがゲンジボタルの学名) / **the Heike firefly** ヘイケボタル(Luciola lateralisがヘイケボタルの学名) / **noteworthy** 特筆すべき / **trait** 特徴 / **periodicity** 周期性 / **luminescence** 発光 / **give off** 発する(光や熱、雰囲気や気体などの場合に使われる) / **whereas** 一方で(＝while, when, where) / **radiate** 放出する / **border** 境界 / **boundary line** 境界線 / **Fossa Magna** フォッサマグナ(地質学で西南日本と東北日本の境目と考えられている断裂帯。Fossa Magnaはラテン語で「大きな溝」という意味) / **central rift zone** 中央地溝帯(大地溝帯とも呼ばれる) / **conjecture** 推測 / **life-altering** 生物を変えるような / **crustal** 地殻の / **genetic engineering** 遺伝子工学 / **gene** 遺伝子

COMPREHENSION

次の英文が本文の内容と一致する場合はT、一致しない場合はFを記入しましょう。

1. (　) The most famous light-emitting animal is the firefly squid.
2. (　) A male Genji firefly in Western Japan emits light once every four seconds.
3. (　) Genji fireflies in Eastern Japan give off light most intensely at 7:45 p.m.
4. (　) The border separating the two different Genji firefly types corresponds to the Fossa Magna.
5. (　) The incorporation of a light-producing gene from fireflies into plants cannot make them radiate light.

Chapter 5 – *Light from Fireflies*

📝 GRAMMAR

次の英文の空所に入れるのに正しい語句を (A) 〜 (D) から選びましょう。

1. Susan got plastic surgery six months ago, so she (　　　) be happy now that she looks far younger than she really is.
   (A) seems to　　(B) seems as　　(C) looks like　　(D) is looked to

2. The head chef was made (　　　) a plan for marketing the new sauce, and as a result of which the small restaurant became more popular.
   (A) form　　(B) to form　　(C) forming　　(D) to be formed

3. My dream is to create an e-marketplace in which people sell and buy the right (　　　) CO_2.
   (A) emits　　(B) emitting　　(C) emitted　　(D) to emit

4. My parents allowed me (　　　) abroad. That is why I have so many American friends.
   (A) study　　(B) studied　　(C) to study　　(D) to be studied

5. It is proper (　　　) the aged and consider helping the poor in modern society.
   (A) of young people to respect　　(B) for young people to respect
   (C) of young people respecting　　(D) for young people respecting

<文法を理解する>　5. 不定詞の用法

不定詞には次の3つの用法があります。
(1) 名詞的用法
　不定詞が文中で主語、目的語、補語になっている場合を名詞的用法と呼びます。
(2) 形容詞的用法
　不定詞が名詞を修飾している場合を形容詞的用法と呼びます。なお、名詞を修飾する場合、修飾される名詞と不定詞の間には、①主格関係（例：a friend to help me「助けてくれる友人」）、②目的格関係（例：a friend to help 「助けてあげる友人」）、③同格関係（例：a promise to write to me every day 「私に毎日手紙を書くという約束」）のいずれかが成立します。
(3) 副詞的用法
　不定詞が動詞を修飾している場合を副詞的用法と呼びます。なお、この用法には、①目的（〜するために）②感情の原因（〜して［うれしいetc.］）③判断の根拠（〜するなんて）④結果（その結果〜する）⑤難易構文（〜するのは）の5つがあるので、これらを正しく識別することが重要です。

COMPOSITION

次の英文の(　　　)内の単語を並べ換えて、意味の通る文にしましょう。

1. It is advisable to take a break for about ten minutes (hours / when / two / once / every) you do work on the computer.
   (　　　　　　　　　　　　　　　　　　　　　　　　　　　　　　　　)

2. One sievert corresponds (100 / amount / to / times / the) of radioactivity exposure expressed by a Roentgen, a unit not in current use.
   (　　　　　　　　　　　　　　　　　　　　　　　　　　　　　　　　)

3. A mathematical way of thinking (to / almost / apply / can / all) fields of science, especially in theoretical physics.
   (　　　　　　　　　　　　　　　　　　　　　　　　　　　　　　　　)

4. The professor I am going to meet today is (brain / on / authority / physiology / an).
   (　　　　　　　　　　　　　　　　　　　　　　　　　　　　　　　　)

5. The malignant (was / from / his / tumor / extracted) body soon after the surgeon opened up his abdomen.
   (　　　　　　　　　　　　　　　　　　　　　　　　　　　　　　　　)

★英語表現の小箱5★　複合語に慣れよう

本文でluminescence-related（発光に関する）という複合形容詞が出てきましたが、ハイフンを用いた複合語は、比較的自由に作ることができます。いくつか挙げてみましょう。

earthquake-proof（耐震の）
earthquake-prone（地震が起こりやすい）
accident-prone（事故を起こしがち[性格/性質]な）
group-oriented（集団志向の）
time-wise（時間的に）
space-wise（空間的に）
snow-covered（雪に覆われた）[=snow-clad]

Chapter 5 – *Light from Fireflies*

🎧 LISTENING & DICTATION   CD 1-11

次の会話を聞いて、空所に単語を埋めましょう。

A: Can I ask you some questions about fireflies? Your name is Hotaru. With a name like (1.   ), I expect you to know at (2.   ) something about fireflies.

B: My mother loves fireflies so she named me Hotaru. And yes, over the years I've come to like them, so ask away.

A: Huh. Interesting. Which are bigger, (3.   ) fireflies or female fireflies? With humans, men are a little taller than women, right? Are fireflies any different?

B: Males are smaller in the (4.   ) of Genji fireflies and Heike fireflies. The Genji males are 15mm long and females are 18mm long, while male Heike fireflies are 8mm long and their females are 10mm long.

A: Is there a (5.   ) difference in the number of male and female fireflies?

B: Yes, males outnumber females. The (6.   ) of males to females is 3 to 1.

A: Well then, in (7.   ) of looking for a mate, male fireflies have a lot of competition.

B: Unfortunately for them, right? It is said that male fireflies (8.   ) females by emitting a strong (9.   ) of light five times in sequence. It's got to be (10.   ) for them to stand out from the crowd, that's for sure.

TIPS 科学よもやま話5　蛍の光

　ホタルの雄は腹部の第6節と第7節の2つを点滅させて、雌に愛のメッセージを送っています。雌も光りますが、第6節のみを輝かせるので、雄よりも光は弱いといえます。

　一般に光を発すると熱も同時に発するものですが、ホタルの光は全く熱くありません。だから「冷光」と呼ばれています。一種の化学反応で発光しているようです。

　風のない蒸し暑い日の夜8時から9時に光を放ちます。この光は、エネルギー効率が高い理想的な光といえますが、その発光メカニズムは複雑で、分からないことも多く、現在も研究されています。

　また、ホタルの光はストレスによる心の病にも効くということが科学的に証明されており、ホタルの光を人工的に再現し、治療に生かす研究も行われています。

CHAPTER 6
Merits and Demerits of Pyramids

古代エジプト王の墓であるピラミッドの建造がアフリカの砂漠化の一因になっていると言えば、信じられるでしょうか。果たして、古代エジプト人のピラミッド建造がもたらした功罪とは…。

◀ VOCABULARY CHECK ▶

次の単語について、その定義を選び結びつけましょう。

1. tomb・　・(A) a structure that serves as a grave
2. desert・　・(B) the lowest part of something; the foundation
3. tool・　・(C) an instrument used to manipulate objects
4. side・　・(D) a large area of land made up of sand
5. base・　・(E) a position or an area to the left or right of something

PASSAGE

CD 1-12

 Do you know the world's three greatest mausoleums? One is the largest of the key hole-shaped tumuli called Nintokutennoryo, which is one of the burial mounds of Mozu located in Sakai City, Osaka, Japan. Another is the first Qin Emperor's tomb famous for its terracotta figures located in Xian City, Shaanxi
5　Province, China. Finally, we have the Great Pyramid of King Khufu located in the midst of the desert in Giza, Egypt.

 The Pyramid of King Khufu is also famous for the discovery of the 43 meter-long wooden "Solar Boat," or "Khufu's Ship," near the pyramid. This Great Pyramid of Giza is also one of the world's three greatest pyramids, the
10　others being Khafre's Pyramid and Menkaure's Pyramid.

 Could it be possible that the building of pyramids contributed to the desertification of Africa?

 In Egypt, there are many pyramids other than the three already mentioned. They are all made of stone bricks or blocks. In appearance it seems that the
15　construction of pyramids is not related to the desertification of Africa, because

wood was not needed. Indeed, it looks as if a large amount of stones were solely used.

In fact, a large amount of wood was needed for the construction of pyramids. The wood was needed to make log rollers or sleighs used to carry stones or to make wedges to split stones or quarry them. So, wood was not used as part of the pyramids themselves but instead used in great amounts as tools for the actual construction. Therefore, people in ancient Egypt continuously lumbered a large tract of forestland.

As a result, the deforested mountains became bare, and ended up being unable to hold groundwater, which contributed to desertification in Africa.

It is true that at the present time pyramids in Egypt play a large role as tourist spots, but the forest lost for the sake of the construction of pyramids may have been too great a price.

Lastly, the fact that the construction of pyramids remains a great mystery even now is noteworthy. For example, the Great Pyramid of Giza was made so meticulously that the division of the entire surface area of its four sides by the area of the base results in the golden number.

NOTES

mausoleum 霊廟 [れいびょう] / **key hole-shaped tumulus** 前方後円墳 (「古墳」という意味の tumulus の複数形が tumuli) / **burial mounds** 古墳群 / **Qin** 秦 (中国の最初の統一王朝) / **terracotta figure** 土で作られた素焼き像 (兵馬俑 [へいばよう] を指す) / **Xian** 西安 [=Xi'an] (陝西省 [せんせいしょう] の省都) / **Shaanxi Province** 陝西省 (中国の行政区画の1つで、山西省と区別するために、英語では Shaanxi Province と表記される) / **King Khufu** クフ王 / **Khafre** カフラー (クフ王の子) / **Menkaure** メンカウラー (カフラーの子) / **desertification** 砂漠化 / **in appearance** 見掛け上 / **log roller** 丸太のコロ (重い物を移動させるときに、下に入れて転がす) / **sleigh** ソリ / **wedge** 楔 [くさび] / **quarry** 切り出す / **lumber a tract of forestland** 森林地帯を伐採する / **deforest** 森林を伐採する / **meticulously** 慎重に / **golden number** 黄金数 (a:b が最も美しいとされる比率の1:1.618を黄金比と呼び、この1.618は2次方程式 $x^2-x-1=0$ の正の解であり、黄金数と呼ばれる)

COMPREHENSION

次の英文が本文の内容と一致する場合はT、一致しない場合はFを記入しましょう。

1. (　) The largest tumulus in Japan is one of the burial mounds of Mozu.
2. (　) The Solar Boat was discovered near the pyramid for Khafre.
3. (　) The building of pyramids is not one of the causes of desertification.
4. (　) A huge amount of stone and wood was used in the building of pyramids.
5. (　) All the mysteries surrounding the pyramids have been unraveled at this time.

GRAMMAR

次の英文の空所に入れるのに正しい語句を (A) 〜 (D) から選びましょう。

1. My boss accepted the bold plan (　　　) by your company.

    (A) proposes　　(B) proposing　　(C) proposed　　(D) to propose

2. I saw my girlfriend cheating on me and a few days later, confronted her about it while (　　　) some questions of her.

    (A) ask　　(B) asking　　(C) asked　　(D) having asked

3. A serious mistake (　　　) by our boss caused my co-worker to turn red in the face.

    (A) mention　　(B) mentions　　(C) mentioning　　(D) mentioned

4. We (　　　) to the mom-and-pop candy store together in order to buy snacks.

    (A) were used to go　　　(B) used going
    (C) used to go　　　(D) used to going

5. When the teacher scolded me, I said, "But … ." Then she stopped me by saying, "Your commentary is (　　　)," so I was left speechless.

    (A) needing　　(B) not needing　　(C) needed　　(D) not needed

＜文法を理解する＞　6. 過去分詞の用法

次の例文について考えてみましょう。

(1) Mary sat <u>surrounded</u> by her children.
（メアリーは子供たちに囲まれて座っていました）

(2) A woman <u>arrested</u> by the police last month died in jail.
（先月警察に逮捕された女性は拘置所で亡くなりました）

過去分詞はbe動詞と結びついて受動態を作ったり、haveと結びついて完了形を作ったりしますが、過去分詞単独では補語になるか名詞を修飾することがあります。上記の例文 (1) ではsurroundedは補語として機能しており、(2) ではarrestedは直前のwomanを修飾しています。

なお、1語の過去分詞が名詞を修飾する際、他動詞派生の過去分詞は「された」という受動の意味を表しますが、自動詞派生の過去分詞は「した」という完了の意味を表すので注意しましょう。例えば、a used carは「使われた車」で「中古車」、a fallen leafは「落ちた葉」で「落ち葉」という意味になります。

Chapter 6 – *Merits and Demerits of Pyramids*

COMPOSITION

次の英文の(　　　)内の単語を並べ換えて、意味の通る文にしましょう。

1. Carbohydrates are one of the three major nutrients, (being / proteins / the / and / others) lipid.
   (　　　　　　　　　　　　　　　　　　　　　　　　　　　　　　　)

2. Repeated animal experiments (being / to / up / unable / ended) show any beneficial effects of the newly developed medicine.
   (　　　　　　　　　　　　　　　　　　　　　　　　　　　　　　　)

3. The sloth is too (us / for / animal / lazy / an) to hope to see one come down from its tree in the daytime.
   (　　　　　　　　　　　　　　　　　　　　　　　　　　　　　　　)

4. What existed before the emergence of time and (great / a / space / mystery / remains) of physics.
   (　　　　　　　　　　　　　　　　　　　　　　　　　　　　　　　)

5. Dr. Jones postulated his new (that / so / theory / it / carefully) may be impervious to criticism from fellow researchers.
   (　　　　　　　　　　　　　　　　　　　　　　　　　　　　　　　)

★英語表現の小箱6★　　used toに似た表現

本文でused to do（…するために用いられた）が出てきましたが、usedを用いた次の表現の違いに注意しましょう。

　　　　used to do　（…したものだ）[過去の規則的な習慣を表す]
　　　　be used to do　（…するために用いられる）[to doは不定詞の副詞的用法]
　　　　be used to doing　（…することに慣れている）[doingは動名詞]
　　　　get used to doing　（…することに慣れる）
　注： would often doも過去の習慣を表しますが、不規則であることを暗示します。

LISTENING & DICTATION

CD 1-13

次の会話を聞いて、空所に単語を埋めましょう。

A: I've been to (1.   ) to see the pyramids. They were fantastic!

B: Are the pyramids the tombs of (2.   ) Egyptian kings?

A: An ancient Egyptian king is called a Pharaoh, and because there are no coffins in the pyramids, they were probably not built as the Pharaohs' (3.   ).

B: Then what are they (4.   )? What do they contribute to?

A: Actually, there are few concrete facts when it (5.   ) to these monuments. However, there is a (6.   ) that the pyramids were a kind of astrological calendar.

B: Then they're only colossal sundials made of stones? Pyramids seem kind of mysterious, like they give (7.   ) a certain power. I feel something even when I look at a picture of them.

A: Actually one legend (8.   ) that after a Pharaoh's death, his spirit travels around the earth on a boat during the night. In the morning, he returns to his pyramid and (9.   ) there. As a result, he is rejuvenated and gains enough power to (10.   ) his flight.

B: That means pyramids are resting places for souls? I wonder how much they charge per night.

TIPS 科学よもやま話6　ピラミッドの石

　最大のピラミッドであるクフ王のピラミッドの石の数は、よく230万個とかいわれていますが、吉村作治氏によると、約300万個のようです。主として石灰岩でできており、その比重から計算すると約600万トンということになります。

　クフ王、カフラー王、メンカウラー王のピラミッドを3大ピラミッドといいますが、そのうち、一番小さなピラミッドであるメンカウラー王のピラミッドは、上部4分の3が白い石灰岩、下部の4分の1が赤い花こう岩と2色に色分けされています。この理由が何であるのかは分かっていません。

　地球と金星の体積の比は1：0.857ですが、これはクフ王のピラミッドとカフラー王のピラミッドの容積の比(1:0.856)にほぼ一致します。カフラー王のピラミッドが金星を象徴していると思われます。このようにピラミッドには不思議がいっぱい詰まっています。

CHAPTER 7

The Birth of the Hawaiian Islands

活火山としても知られる山、富士山。過去にどのような火山活動があったのでしょうか。また、火山は陸だけでなく海にもあり、海底火山は時として島になることもあります。そこで、ハワイ諸島はどのようにして生まれたのか考えてみましょう。

◀ VOCABULARY CHECK ▶

次の単語について、その定義を選び結びつけましょう。

1. picturesque・ ・(A) main; most important; first
2. volcanic ・ ・(B) caused or produced by a volcano
3. attributable・ ・(C) happening or doing something often
4. frequent ・ ・(D) probably caused by the thing mentioned
5. prime ・ ・(E) pretty, especially in a charming way

PASSAGE

CD 1-14

Japan is home to many mountains. For example, among the most interesting mountains in Japan is Mt. Tempo located in Osaka. It is known as the lowest mountain at only 4.53 meters high. The most famous mountain in Japan is Mt. Fuji, which is Japan's highest mountain. It was designated as a World Heritage Site by UNESCO in 2013.

Some may see Mt. Fuji as simply a beautiful or picturesque mountain, but it is important to remember that it is actually an active volcano. In fact, Mt. Fuji has erupted several times in the past. Its most well-known event was the Hoei Great Eruption, which occurred in 1707. The eruption was so massive that volcanic ash covered the entire town of Edo.

Incidentally, we often think of volcanoes as situated only on land; however, volcanoes exist under the sea as well. Undersea volcanoes often erupt on a smaller scale compared with volcanoes on land. These small-scale eruptions are due to high water pressure attributable to the huge amount of seawater enveloping them.

If an eruption occurs in relatively shallow waters, they sometimes have as great an impact as volcanoes on land. For example, the series of eruptions that occurred off the coast of Nishino-shima of the Ogasawara Islands on November 20, 2013, was so great that a new island was created. This nascent island has been increasing in size month by month and has formed into a shape that looks like Snoopy. It's anyone's guess when the island will stop growing, but in the meantime watching it develop is exciting.

If volcanic activity is frequent and of high magnitude, submerged volcanoes may form volcanic islands after their summits rise above the ocean. The Hawaiian Islands are a prime example of this phenomenon.

The Hawaiian Islands consist of 19 islands and atolls. The 8 main islands are Hawai'i, Maui, Kaho'olawe, Lana'i, Moloka'i, O'ahu, Kaua'i, and Ni'ihau from south to north. This order also reflects the ages of the islands. The present Hawaiian Islands were established as a result of a northwestern migration of the islands, formed out of a magma jet. This jet is referred to as a "hotspot" located in the southeastern sea off the coast of Hawai'i Island (the largest and southernmost island). The islands birthed by the eruption were subsequently moved along on the crustal plate to their current-day positions.

NOTES

be designated as a World Heritage Site 世界遺産に指定されている / **active volcano** 活火山 / **erupt** 噴火する / **massive** 大規模の / **volcanic ash** 火山灰 / **envelop** 覆う / **shallow water** 浅瀬 / **off the coast of ~** ～沖で / **nascent** 初期の / **submerged** 海面下の / **summit** 頂上 / **prime example** 最たるもの / **atoll** 環礁(環状のサンゴ礁) / **Hawai'i, Maui, Kaho'olawe, Lana'i, Moloka'i, O'ahu, Kaua'i, and Ni'ihau** ハワイ島、マウイ島、カホオラウェ島、ラナイ島、モロカイ島、オアフ島、カウアイ島、ニイハウ島 / **reflect** 表す / **magma jet** マグマの噴流 / **hotspot** ホットスポット(マグマの火山活動が起こる場所) / **birth** [米]生み出す / **crustal plate** 地殻プレート

COMPREHENSION

次の英文が本文の内容と一致する場合はT、一致しない場合はFを記入しましょう。

1. (　) The lowest mountain in Japan is located in Osaka Prefecture.
2. (　) Mt. Fuji had a large scale eruption in 1707.
3. (　) The eruptions of undersea volcanoes are always smaller than those of volcanoes on land.
4. (　) Nishino-shima Island is in the shape of Snoopy.
5. (　) The Hawaiian Islands were formed from a so-called magma jet.

Chapter 7 – *The Birth of the Hawaiian Islands*

GRAMMAR

次の英文の空所に入れるのに正しい語句を(A) 〜 (D)から選びましょう。

1. My mother served as principal of the school (　　　　) in the neighboring city.
   (A) locate　　(B) locating　　(C) located　　(D) to locate

2. There was a beautiful lily (　　　　) the flowers in the vase on the table.
   (A) among　　(B) within　　(C) inside　　(D) from

3. We are going to hold Mary's birthday party tomorrow; however, she dislikes Jack, so she may go out somewhere if he (　　　　).
   (A) come　　(B) comes　　(C) came　　(D) will come

4. Hal sings so beautifully (　　　　) I can't believe he was eliminated from the singing competition.
   (A) as　　(B) since　　(C) that　　(D) unless

5. Isabella is a very good dancer; (　　　　) her dance really moves me.
   (A) watch　　(B) watches　　(C) watched　　(D) watching

＜文法を理解する＞　7. 多義語のas

asには次の用法があります。それぞれに習熟して使いこなせるようにしましょう。
　(1) 接続詞
①時(〜の時)、②理由(〜なので)、③比例(〜につれて)、④様態(〜のように)、⑤譲歩(〜だけれども)、⑥前出の名詞限定(〜のような)という6つの意味があります。
　(2) 前置詞
通常は「〜として」「〜のような」という意味を表しますが、regard A as BのようにBが補語であることを明示する際にも使われます。
　(3) 関係代名詞
制限用法では先行詞にas / so / such / the sameが付く場合に用いられ、非制限用法の場合は主節全体や主節の一部を先行詞とすることができます。
　(4) 副詞
「同じくらい」という意味で、原級比較のas 〜 as …という表現の前のasがこれにあたります(なお、後ろのasは接続詞です)。

✎ COMPOSITION

次の英文の(　　　)内の単語を並べ換えて、意味の通る文にしましょう。

1. Wind power is sufficient if you need (small / on / scale / electricity / a), but for an entire nation, it is not enough.
   (　　　　　　　　　　　　　　　　　　　　　　　　　　　　　　　　　　　)

2. The researcher (by / investigated / month / how / month) the cancer cells developed in the mouse's body.
   (　　　　　　　　　　　　　　　　　　　　　　　　　　　　　　　　　　　)

3. The technology related to iPS cells was an (towards / of / magnitude / event / great) the advancement of Japanese medicine.
   (　　　　　　　　　　　　　　　　　　　　　　　　　　　　　　　　　　　)

4. As (of / a / the / result / investigation) conducted last month by their team, a new theory was put forward.
   (　　　　　　　　　　　　　　　　　　　　　　　　　　　　　　　　　　　)

5. The fisherman used to fish three (coast / off / of / kilometers / the) the sparsely populated island.
   (　　　　　　　　　　　　　　　　　　　　　　　　　　　　　　　　　　　)

★英語表現の小箱7★　「美しい」を意味する表現

本文にpicturesque（美しい）が出てきましたが、「美しい」を意味する英語は多くあります。

- good-looking; attractive; charming; comely; lovesome; eye-filling
- 声が美しい⇒　sweet (voice)
- 街並みが美しい⇒　orderly (streets)
- 心が美しい⇒　pure (heart)

参考：彼女は心が美しい。→ She really has a heart of gold.
　　　　　　　　　　　　[=She really has a sweet nature.]

Chapter 7 – *The Birth of the Hawaiian Islands*

🎧 LISTENING & DICTATION   CD 1-15

次の会話を聞いて、空所に単語を埋めましょう。

A: I hear you've been to Hawaii, right?

B: Yes, it really is a beautiful place. I had the (1.   ) to visit the Hawaii Volcanoes National Park, (2.   ) is designated as a World Heritage Site. It's (3.   ) for its Kilauea. By the way, do you know how the Hawaiian Islands came into (4.   )?

A: By volcanic activity? I've heard submerged volcanoes erupted and the volcanoes (5.   ) above the sea, producing the islands one after another.

B: Yeah, this kind of underwater volcanic activity seems to have (6.   ) about 25 million years ago.

A: The Hawaiian Islands consist of eight islands, right? On the map, the islands (7.   ) up from the northwestern end to the southeastern tip. Which island is older, the northwestern island or the southeastern island?

B: The northwestern one. The islands (8.   ) in a southeasterly direction. But the Pacific plate on which the islands lie seems to be moving in the opposite direction from the islands' formation. I read this plate is approaching Japan at a (9.   ) of about 6 centimeters each year.

A: So, someday in the future we'll be able to see Hawaii from Japan? When?

B: Don't (10.   ) your breath; it will take about 100 million years.

TIPS 科学よもやま話7　ハワイ諸島

　ハワイ諸島は、2,560kmにキロにわたって北西方向に点在する、8つの大きな島と124の小さな島から成り立っています。北西にいくほど古くなり、最も古い島は、北西端にあるクレ環礁で、約3,000万年前に誕生しています。

　さらに北西方向に水没した火山が連なっており、ハワイ海山群を形成しています。これは4,000万年前以降に形成された海山群で、西北西に延びています。

　さらにその先は、北北西に延びる海山群があり、天皇海山群と呼ばれています。こちらの海山は4,000万年以前に生まれたもので、日本の天皇の名前が付けられています。例えば、新しいものから順に、主なものを示すと、桓武海山(約4,000万年前)、応神海山(約5,500万年前)、推古海山(約6,500万年前)、明治海山(約8,200万年前)などがあります。

CHAPTER 8
Bees and the Extinction of Man

ヒトはさまざまな点でミツバチから恩恵を受けていますが、ミツバチはどのような生き物なのでしょうか。また、世界各国でCCDという現象が報告されていますが、これはどのような現象なのでしょうか。

◀ VOCABULARY CHECK ▶

次の単語について、その定義を選び結びつけましょう。

1. contribution・   ・(A) the facts about something
2. shortage・   ・(B) the state of continuing to live or exist
3. combination・   ・(C) a sum of money given to help pay for something
4. truth・   ・(D) two or more things joined or mixed together
5. survival・   ・(E) a situation in which there is not enough of something

PASSAGE

CD 1-16

    In the animal kingdom, female bees carry one of the heaviest burdens. Male bees get their food from the efforts of the exclusively female worker bees without any contributions. Therefore, the English word "drone," which refers to a male bee, also means a lazy and mindless person.

5   The ecology of bees is wondrous. Only female bees are born from fertilized eggs, and the only female raised by royal jelly rich in nutrition can grow to be a queen bee, which is able to mate and spawn eggs. The female bees that do not qualify to be queens live off pollen and honey as worker bees. Male bees are born from unfertilized eggs.

10   The queen bee is two to three times bigger and lives 30 to 40 times longer than worker bees, and spawns about 1,500 eggs every day; worker bees cannot create eggs.

    Human beings are blessed with some extraordinarily useful things from bees. Besides honey, which can be used as food or added to cosmetics, the main
15 substances they provide us are beeswax, which can be used for wax, soap and candles, and propolis or royal jelly used for health foods.

A troubling phenomenon causing the mass death of bees has been confirmed in Europe, the United States, India, Brazil, as well as other countries. This potentially devastating problem, which started in the U.S. in 2006, is called CCD (Colony Collapse Disorder or Inai-inai disease in Japan). In Japan, there has been a shortage of bees but it has not been proven if the shortage is linked to CCD.

There are many theories why CCD occurs. There's a theory revolving around malnutrition and another concerned with a possible new type of mite. One states it is related to agricultural chemicals, yet another attributes it to genetically modified crops. There is even a theory that says that electromagnetic force is to blame. The most agreed-on theory is the stress-stricken theory, which posits that bees' immune system is weakened due to a combination of several factors.

There is an urban legend that says that humans will go extinct in 4 years if all bees disappear from the earth. Since bees are closely related to pollination, plants will be doomed and the impact on all life will be the severest. However, the truth regarding these consequences is not known at the moment. At any rate, it is clear that bees contribute to the survival of human beings to at least some extent.

NOTES

worker bee 働き蜂 / **mindless** 愚かな / **ecology** 生態 / **wondrous** 不思議な / **fertilized egg** 受精卵 / **mate** 交尾する / **spawn** 産む / **qualify to be ~** 〜の要件を満たす / **live off** 〜だけを食べて生きる / **pollen** 花粉 / **unfertilized egg** 無精卵 / **be blessed with ~** 〜に恵まれている / **beeswax** 蜜蝋(ミツバチの巣を構成する蝋を精製したもの) / **propolis** プロポリス(ミツバチが集めた樹脂製混合物) / **CCD** 蜂群崩壊症候群(大量のミツバチが巣箱で死んでいたり、突然巣箱からミツバチの群れがいなくなる現象) / **revolve around ~** 〜を中心に展開する / **malnutrition** 栄養失調 / **mite** ダニ / **genetically modified crop** 遺伝子組み換え作物(modifiedの代わりにengineeredやalteredが使われることもある) / **electromagnetic force** 電磁力 / **agreed-on** 認められた / **stress-stricken** ストレスに打ちひしがれた / **posit** 仮定する / **immune system** 免疫システム / **go extinct** 絶滅する / **doom** 滅亡させる

COMPREHENSION

次の英文が本文の内容と一致する場合はT、一致しない場合はFを記入しましょう。

1. (　) Worker bees are all males.
2. (　) Male bees are not born from fertilized eggs.
3. (　) The queen bee lives two to three times longer than a worker bee.
4. (　) The reason for the lack of bees in Japan is clearly due to CCD.
5. (　) According to an urban legend, 4 years after the disappearance of bees, humans may go extinct.

GRAMMAR

次の英文の空所に入れるのに正しい語句を (A) ～ (D) から選びましょう。

1. I was approached by a stranger asking directions so I missed the train and (　　　) was late for school.
   (A) also　　　(B) but　　　(C) for　　　(D) therefore

2. Most of our classmates dislike Nancy because she is mean, (　　　) I like her.
   (A) so　　　(B) but　　　(C) however　　　(D) since

3. We saw Sam for the first time in ten years. He was not fat, (　　　) he was surely getting there.
   (A) and　　　(B) yet　　　(C) hence　　　(D) however

4. (　　　) we are all working overtime tonight, you should also stay and help us.
   (A) For　　　(B) Since　　　(C) That　　　(D) Though

5. It was Mr. Watanabe (　　　) I met at Osaka Station. I was surprised because I hadn't heard from him for about three years.
   (A) that　　　(B) this　　　(C) which　　　(D) whether

＜文法を理解する＞　8. 等位接続詞と従位接続詞

接続詞には等位接続詞と従位接続詞の2つがあります。前者の等位接続詞には、語と語、句と句、節と節を結び付けるという働きがあり、後者の従位接続詞には従節を主節につなげるという働きがあります（なお、従位接続詞に導かれる節は名詞節か副詞節となります）。

> The real cause of our company's bankruptcy is not clear but the first indicator was the dismissal of five workmen.

等しい関係にあるもの同士を結び付ける等位接続詞の働きは、相関表現の場合にも当てはまります。しかし、上記英文で使われている表現はnot A but B（AでなくB）という相関表現でしょうか。もしそう考えると、clearという語とthe first indicator was the dismissal of five workmenという節が結び付いていることになってしまいます。従って、ここでは相関表現ではなく単に否定文と肯定文をbutがつないでいただけということになります。見慣れた表現でも、基本に忠実であることが大切です。なお、例文は「我が社の倒産の真相は不明ですが、そのきっかけは5人の従業員の解雇でした」という意味です。

Chapter 8 – *Bees and the Extinction of Man*

✏️ COMPOSITION

次の英文の(　　)内の単語を並べ換えて、意味の通る文にしましょう。

1. The diameter of the star Betelgeuse is (to / larger / times / two / three) than it was about 40 years ago.
   (　　　　　　　　　　　　　　　　　　　　　　　　　　　　　　　)

2. Her master's program's professors delivered lectures (were / to / interesting / extraordinarily / that) her.
   (　　　　　　　　　　　　　　　　　　　　　　　　　　　　　　　)

3. Dr. Shibazaburo Kitazato is known for his work in vaccinations as (in / well / success / as / his) creating a pure culture of tetanus bacilli.
   (　　　　　　　　　　　　　　　　　　　　　　　　　　　　　　　)

4. The Japanese river otter is said to (because / extinct / have / it / gone) has not been seen since 1979.
   (　　　　　　　　　　　　　　　　　　　　　　　　　　　　　　　)

5. The experiment conducted yesterday was successful to (after / results / some / the / extent) led to three of the initial problems being resolved.
   (　　　　　　　　　　　　　　　　　　　　　　　　　　　　　　　)

★英語表現の小箱8★　　＜go＋形容詞＞の表現

本文でgo extinct（絶滅する）が出てきましたが、＜go＋形容詞＞の表現はマイナスイメージが多いと言えます。いくつか注意すべきものを挙げておきましょう。

　　go bad（腐る）
　　go sour（[人間関係などが]こじれる）
　　go blind（目が見えなくなる）
　　go gray（髪が白くなる）
　　go bankrupt（倒産する）[=go into bankruptcy]

LISTENING & DICTATION

次の会話を聞いて、空所に単語を埋めましょう。

A: A beehive is certainly a wondrous (1.   ).

B: What do you mean?

A: One hive is (2.   ) up of only one bee that qualifies to be a queen. There are several (3.   ) or fewer male bees, and some thousands to tens of thousands of worker bees, (4.   ) are all female. They fly about (5.   ) for honey within a four-kilometer radius from the hive.

B: How much honey does a bee (6.   ) during its lifetime?

A: It's said that one honey bee harvests only one spoonful of honey in its entire life. The bee makes a tremendous effort to gather this honey, fending off attacks from its (7.   ) enemies: birds, spiders and frogs.

B: I see, but a honey bee is still a bee. They can (8.   ) just like a hornet, right?

A: It can use its stinger, but rarely does. Once it stings a human or another animal, its abdomen is (9.   ) open when the stinger breaks off and ends up causing the bee to bleed to death. Whether or not to sting something is not a decision to be taken lightly.

B: Wow, it kind of sounds like an (10.   ) legend! Bees sure have a rough life, don't they?

TIPS 科学よもやま話8　ミツバチ2話

　1．かわいそうな雄蜂：雄蜂は交尾のみが仕事のようです。そしてかわいそうな運命をたどります。晴れの日を選んで集団で飛び立ち、その群れに女王蜂が飛び込んで交尾を行い、女王蜂は巣に帰り産卵を開始します。交尾した雄蜂は腹部を破壊されるので死亡し、交尾できなかった雄も巣にもどりますが、繁殖期を終えると、働き蜂に巣を追い出され、死亡します。

　2．すごいミツバチのチームワーク：ミツバチの天敵であるスズメバチを蒸し殺す技に目を見張るものがあります。巣の中に侵入したスズメバチを多くのミツバチが取り囲み蜂球（ほうきゅう）という塊を作り、その中で20分間48度の熱で蒸し殺すのです。スズメバチの致死温度が44〜46度で、ミツバチは48度〜50度なので、ミツバチが死ぬことはほとんどありません。

CHAPTER 9

Herbivorous Horns

ウシ、サイ、シカ、キリン、ヤギは角のある動物ですが、一言で「角」といってもそれぞれに異なった特徴があります。それは何なのでしょうか。また、なぜ草食動物には角が生えているのでしょうか。

◀ VOCABULARY CHECK ▶

次の単語について、その定義を選び結びつけましょう。

1. feature · · (A) to show something to someone
2. expose · · (B) an important social or religious event
3. exhibit · · (C) to show something that is usually hidden
4. ceremony · · (D) to make someone interested in something
5. attract · · (E) something important or typical of a place or thing

PASSAGE

　How do you answer the following question? What are two common features shared by oxen, rhinoceroses, deer, giraffes and goats? One is that they are plant-eating animals. The other is the fact that they all have horns.

　The horns of an ox are made of bone covered by keratin, while the horn of a rhinoceros consists solely of keratin. Therefore, a rhino's horn can regenerate even if it is broken, while a bone horn can't.

　The horns of a deer, called antlers, and of a giraffe, ossicones, are made of skin-covered bone. The bone of the deer is actually exposed through its antler's skin in autumn. From all these examples, we can see that the structure of horns slightly differs from animal to animal.

　Interestingly, the goat has a horn that is warm compared with that of the deer. This is because the goat's horn contains cerebrospinal fluid. Therefore, a goat experiences pain when its horn is damaged. This is manifested by the signs of physical distress that a goat exhibits when its horn is being cut. In contrast, the cutting of a deer's horns won't hurt the animal; therefore, a deer-horn cutting ceremony takes place in Nara. It is worth noting that a goat's horns bend backwards. This points to the fact that they are not meant to be used aggressively.

Unlike herbivores, carnivores do not have horns. The horns of herbivores also have various uses. In general, horns perform one or more of the following functions:

(1) As a defensive tool to protect the animal from its natural predators
(2) As an ornament to attract females
(3) As an instrument for foraging food
(4) To display their status in a group
(5) To make it burdensome for a natural enemy to eat their carcasses after they are attacked

Grass-eating animals are doomed to the role of prey for meat-eating animals. In that sense, they are weak and must rely on their horns for at least some protection. When considering this, would it make sense for physically weak humans to have horns in order to protect against stronger humans?

NOTES

herbivorous 草食性の / **oxen**（「牛」という意味のoxの複数形）/ **rhinoceros** サイ（略式ではrhinoと表記される）/ **deer** シカ（通例は単複同形）/ **giraffe** キリン / **goat** ヤギ / **keratin** 角質 / **regenerate** 再生する / **antler** アントラー（シカの角）/ **ossicones** オッシコーン（キリンの角）/ **cerebrospinal fluid** 脳脊髄液（略称はCSFで、脳室系とクモ膜下腔を満たす無色透明の液体。略して髄液とも）/ **manifest** 証明する / **distress** 苦痛 / **in contrast** 対照的に（= by way of contrast）/ **aggressively** 攻撃的に / **herbivore** 草食動物 / **carnivore** 肉食動物 / **one or more** 1つ以上 / **natural predator** 天敵 / **ornament** 装身具 / **forage (for) food** 食べ物を調達する / **carcass** 死骸 / **be doomed to ~** ～の運命にある / **prey** 獲物

COMPREHENSION

次の英文が本文の内容と一致する場合はT、一致しない場合はFを記入しましょう。

1. (　) A rhinoceros's horns can regenerate if cut off.
2. (　) Deer horns consist of bone covered with keratin.
3. (　) Since a goat's horn has cerebrospinal fluid, it is warmer than a deer's.
4. (　) One of the reasons herbivores have horns is to protect themselves from their natural enemies.
5. (　) Most male herbivores have horns solely for fighting against competing males.

Chapter 9 – *Herbivorous Horns*

GRAMMAR

次の英文の空所に入れるのに正しい語句を (A) ～ (D) から選びましょう。

1. It sure is a shame (　　　) you can't take part in our theatrical circle.
   (A) that　　(B) which　　(C) what　　(D) therefore

2. Do you think there is any likelihood (　　　) he will be successful in his new venture?
   (A) if　　(B) that　　(C) what　　(D) which

3. Now this is a person (　　　) I think is very smart; therefore, I want to meet him some day in the future.
   (A) whose　　(B) whom　　(C) which　　(D) that

4. The population of the city is about one fourth as large as (　　　) of Tokyo.
   (A) one　　(B) that　　(C) those　　(D) it

5. Your target audience is one of the most important things that (　　　) have to bear in mind when speaking in public.
   (A) who　　(B) you　　(C) would　　(D) is why

＜文法を理解する＞　9. 多機能の that

that には次の用法があります。それぞれに習熟して使いこなせるようにしましょう。

(1) 関係詞
　　関係代名詞としても、関係副詞としても使われます。

(2) 接続詞
　　名詞節を導く場合は主語、目的語、補語、同格として機能します。また、副詞節を導く場合は、①判断の根拠（～するとは）、②程度・結果(so ~ that …で程度や結果の意味)、③目的・結果(so that ~ で目的や結果、in order that ~ で目的の意味)を表します。なお、so that ~ には結果の意味を表す場合もあります)の3つの場合があります。

(3) 強調構文
　　It is ~ that... という形で強調構文を作ります。

(4) 代名詞・形容詞・副詞
　　代名詞の場合は自分から離れているものを指し、形容詞の場合は「あの～、その～」、副詞の場合は「それほど～」という意味になります。

COMPOSITION

次の英文の（　　）内の単語を並べ換えて、意味の通る文にしましょう。

1. Lesser pandas, or red pandas, do (the / not / bear / to / belong / family), though giant pandas do.
   (　　　　　　　　　　　　　　　　　　　　　　　　　　　　　　　　)

2. (with / that / India / elephants / inhabit / compared), African elephants have larger ears and are subject to violent changes of mood.
   (　　　　　　　　　　　　　　　　　　　　　　　　　　　　　　　　)

3. It is (have / noting / no / that / lions / worth) tooth decay; therefore, the word Lion was used for the toothpaste manufacturing company.
   (　　　　　　　　　　　　　　　　　　　　　　　　　　　　　　　　)

4. All the phenomena related to young men's (behavior / the / point / that / to / fact) they are getting more and more feminine.
   (　　　　　　　　　　　　　　　　　　　　　　　　　　　　　　　　)

5. I think repeated experiments will (possible / for / researchers / it / make / us) to confirm that the hypothesis is correct.
   (　　　　　　　　　　　　　　　　　　　　　　　　　　　　　　　　)

★英語表現の小箱9★　　contrastに似た単語あれこれ

本文でcontrast（対照）という単語が出てきました。
contrastのつづりに似た単語に注意しましょう。
　　contract（契約）
　　contact（接触）→ contact+人（人に連絡を取る）[＜contact with 人＞にしない]
日本語訳の「対照」と同じ音の英単語にも注意しましょう。
　　「対象」object
　　「対称」symmetry →「非対称」はasymmetry

Chapter 9 – *Herbivorous Horns*

🎧 LISTENING & DICTATION   CD 1-19

次の会話を聞いて、空所に単語を埋めましょう。

A: You know giraffes have (1.   ), right?

B: Do they? Oh, that's right! They do, don't they? I remember (2.   ) some small knobs on their heads.

A: Do you know how many horns they have?

B: I never (3.   ) that much attention.

A: They have five horns. Two are on (4.   ) of the head; one is between their eyes; and the (5.   ) two are on the back of the head.

B: With most animals, only the male has horns. I think this is because a male has to fight rivals to (6.   ) a female. At the very least, this has got to be one of the reasons for animal horns.

A: That's right, but in the case of a giraffe, both males and females (7.   ) horns. The two horns on the top are there for fighting, to do (8.   ) to their enemies. However, the (9.   ) horns carry no specific significance. They seem to be vestigial, left over from earlier in the giraffes' (10.   ).

B: Oh, kind of like the human appendix and tailbone then.

TIPS 科学よもやま話9　動物の角

　草食動物のみならず、他の動物にも角があります。例えば、昆虫では、カブトムシなど角を持つものが存在します。カブトムシは、動物**界**節足動物**門**昆虫**綱**甲虫**目**コガネムシ**科**カブトムシ**属**に属します。カブトムシの角は、雄同士の争いや、餌をめぐって他の昆虫を追い払うために使われます。

　カブトムシと人気を二分するクワガタムシ（甲虫目クワガタムシ科）の角は、実は大きな顎［あご］です。また、角が童謡で歌われているカタツムリの2本の角は、実は触角で、その先には目が付いています。この目は明暗を感じる程度のものです。カタツムリにはもう1対の小触角がありますが、こちらは味覚と嗅覚を担当しています。

CHAPTER 10
Sunflowers and the Sun!?

夏を代表する花、ヒマワリ。ヒマワリが持つ花言葉とは何でしょうか。ヒマワリは太陽の方角を向く植物として有名ですが、どのようなメカニズムでヒマワリは太陽の後を追うのでしょうか。

◀ VOCABULARY CHECK ▶

次の単語について、その定義を選び結びつけましょう。

1. bloom •   • (A) to make flowers appear or open
2. derive •   • (B) to search for something by following the marks it leaves
3. track •   • (C) to come or develop from something
4. appear •   • (D) to be seen as something or to be present
5. face •   • (E) to deal with a difficult situation

PASSAGE

CD 1-20

    A phrase that attaches a symbolic meaning to flowers is called "the language of flowers." As seen in the sentence "the language of roses is love," attributing a flower to a word, a phrase or emotion is quite common. In many cultures of the world, we find traditions in which a flower is given a symbolic meaning.

5   The present custom of attaching meaning to flowers was at its height in Europe during the 19th century. This trend was introduced to Japan in the beginning of the Meiji era. Originally, the European custom was followed closely with a language of flowers unique to Japan.

    Some examples of this poetic use of language are "honor" for laurel trees, 10 "the pure and simple heart of maidens" for cosmoses, and "don't forget me" for forget-me-nots. Only the sunflower carries the message "I only have eyes for you."

    Sunflowers grow to a height of about three meters tall with large yellow flowers that bloom in summer. The Chinese characters used for the Japanese name of this flower are said to have derived from the fact that the flower turns around toward the direction of the sun, following its movement.

The way that sunflowers track the sun is interesting. From their budding stages and earlier, they bend toward the east in the morning, stand straight up at noon, and bow toward the west in the evening. However, around the time of blooming, these actions cease. So basically, bending towards the sun is deeply related to the growth of sunflowers before blooming.

Until their budding stage, the part of their stalks that sunlight doesn't reach grows larger. As a result, sunflowers appear to be leaning towards the sun. In short, we can say that the flowers do not grow just because they face the sun; the fact is that because they grow, they look as if they face the sun.

This phenomenon does not apply only to sunflowers. In fact, other flowers also face towards the sun. Compared to them, sunflowers in particular are so big that we pay more attention to their behavior.

NOTES

sunflower ヒマワリ / **attach** 結びつける / **symbolic** 象徴的な / **height** 絶頂 / **originally** 当初は（＝at first）/ **closely** きっちりと / **honor** 栄光 / **laurel tree** 月桂樹（laurelだけでも「月桂樹」という意味になる）/ **the pure and simple heart of maidens** 乙女の純真 / **forget-me-not** 忘れな草 / **Chinese character** 漢字（ここでは「向日葵」(ヒマワリ)という漢字を暗示）/ **track** 跡を追う / **budding** 蕾[つぼみ]を出しかけた / **stalk** 茎 / **lean** 傾く

COMPREHENSION

次の英文が本文の内容と一致する場合はT、一致しない場合はFを記入しましょう。

1. ( ) In the language of flowers, forget-me-nots represent honor.
2. ( ) The large yellow blossoms of sunflowers bloom in summer.
3. ( ) Sunflowers face the direction of the sun in all stages of their growth.
4. ( ) The part of sunflowers' stalks that are exposed to the sun grows larger than the part in the shade.
5. ( ) Sunflowers are the only flower that seems to track the sun.

GRAMMAR

次の英文の空所に入れるのに正しい語句を (A) 〜 (D) から選びましょう。

1. The teacher told everyone to bring (　　　) English-Japanese dictionaries.
   (A) they　　　(B) their　　　(C) them　　　(D) theirs

2. There are not so (　　　) parents who know the amount of time their children spend studying.
   (A) many　　　(B) much　　　(C) little　　　(D) as to

3. (　　　) students at the university don't know how to address their professors properly.
   (A) Any　　　(B) Any of　　　(C) Some　　　(D) Some of

4. In the shopping mall, (　　　) enjoyed shopping and others just walked around.
   (A) all　　　(B) much　　　(C) some　　　(D) ones

5. What I want to say is (　　　). In your day and age, you should study hard.
   (A) it　　　(B) this　　　(C) that　　　(D) what

<文法を理解する>　10. 相関的に用いる不定代名詞

相関的に用いる不定代名詞では、次の点がポイントとなります。
(1) 2者・2物の場合

どちらか一方がone、残ったもう一方がthe otherとなります。
(2) 3者・3物以上の場合

①A〜Jの中で、ランダムでどれか1つを指す場合はone、次にoneで指したもの以外をランダムで1つ指す場合はanotherとなります。
②A〜Jの中で、いくつか(仮にA〜E)をまとめて指す場合はsome、次に残ったもの全て(F〜J)をまとめて指す場合はthe othersとなります。
③A〜Jの中で、いくつか(仮にA〜C)をまとめて指す場合はsome、次に残ったD〜Jの中でいくつか(仮にG〜I)をまとめて指す場合はsomeまたはothersとなります。

Chapter 10 – *Sunflowers and the Sun!?*

COMPOSITION

次の英文の（　　　）内の単語を並べ換えて、意味の通る文にしましょう。

1. Cherry blossoms are usually (their / in / beginning / the / peak / at) of April in Japan.
   (　　　　　　　　　　　　　　　　　　　　　　　　　　　　　　　　　　)

2. The rings (not / that / unique / surround / are / Saturn) to Saturn; it has been confirmed that Uranus, Jupiter and Neptune also have them.
   (　　　　　　　　　　　　　　　　　　　　　　　　　　　　　　　　　　)

3. Sequoias, which belong to the cedar family of the pine order, often (over / grow / of / to / height / a) 100 meters.
   (　　　　　　　　　　　　　　　　　　　　　　　　　　　　　　　　　　)

4. There is one (that / book / may / in / help / particular) you in your research into the history of the universe.
   (　　　　　　　　　　　　　　　　　　　　　　　　　　　　　　　　　　)

5. We should pay (the / attention / where / to / situation / more) large amounts of various kinds of space debris are revolving around the earth.
   (　　　　　　　　　　　　　　　　　　　　　　　　　　　　　　　　　　)

★英語表現の小箱１０★　「注目する」の英語表現

本文でpay attention to 〜（〜に注目する）が出てきましたが、これを意味する英語表現も豊富にあります。いくつか挙げてみましょう。

　　　direct one's attention to 〜 [=turn one's attention to 〜]
　　　take note of 〜 [=take notice of 〜]
　　　keep one's eye upon 〜

参考：一語の単語であるwatch、observe、mark、remarkなども「注目する」の意味があります。

LISTENING & DICTATION

次の会話を聞いて、空所に単語を埋めましょう。

A: You like morning glories. What kinds of meanings are (1.   ) to this flower?

B: Well, among others, "fleeting love" and "enduring love." The short time in which the flower (2.   ) in the morning is suggestive of love that is short-lived. However, the thick vines of this flower are (3.   ) of strength, which carries the message of a powerful, enduring love. I prefer the latter message, of course.

A: This flower is not (4.   ) to Japan, is it? Do you know when it came to Japan?

B: It was introduced between the end of the Nara period and the beginning of the Heian period from China. In China, it was (5.   ) as medicine. It is said that if received as a gift by someone, the recipient would visit the gift-giver with a (6.   ) as an offer of thanks. Because of this, the morning glory was once called the "cow-pulling flower."

A: Today this flower is for showing appreciation, right?

B: It was during the Edo period that it started to be cultivated to symbolize appreciation. Since then a wide (7.   ) of species has been grown. The morning glory is a unique garden plant in the sense that it has (8.   ) kinds of flowers.

A: I had no idea the morning glory was so interesting.

B: The tea master Rikyu is said to have placed a solitary morning glory in the altar of his tea room so elegantly that Toyotomi Hideyoshi was (9.   ) by the beauty of the flower. It is said that Rikyu plucked every morning glory in his garden and disposed of them. He put only one in his room to (10.   ) the spirit of the tea ceremony. This story is fascinating.

TIPS 科学よもやま話10　コスモスの花言葉

　コスモスの一般的に有名な花言葉は、「乙女の真心」または「乙女の純真」です。しかし、このコスモスは色によって花言葉が異なります。例えば、白いコスモスは「乙女の純潔」「優美」という意味を持っています。赤いコスモスは「乙女の愛情」「調和」という意味があります。従って、白と赤のコスモスの中間であるピンクのコスモスは、「乙女の純潔」と「乙女の愛情」の2つの花言葉が存在しています。

　黄色いコスモスは「野生の美しさ」、黒いコスモスは「恋の終わり」が花言葉のようです。

CHAPTER 11
Trees of Greatness and the Greatness of Trees

世界にはたくさんの木があります。その中でも、5つの興味深い木について紹介しましょう。また、ヒトは森からたくさんの恩恵を受けていますが、森が生み出すきれいな空気と水をヒトが作り出そうと思えば一体どれほどの費用がかかるのでしょうか。

◀ VOCABULARY CHECK ▶

次の単語について、その定義を選び結びつけましょう。

1. characterize・ ・(A) a supply of something that people can use
2. classify・ ・(B) to try very hard to achieve something
3. beneficial・ ・(C) having a good effect
4. resource・ ・(D) to describe the qualities of someone or something
5. strive・ ・(E) to arrange something in groups according to features

PASSAGE

There are some great trees in the world. Among them are some especially noteworthy trees that deserve to be seen at least once in our lifetime.

First, the dragon's blood tree is extraordinary for its blood red sap. It can be found on Socotra Island in Yemen. This tree has been used as medicine and dyestuff since the age of the ancient Roman Empire. It is characterized by its crowded branches bent upward, which look quite amazing.

Secondly, a giant tree called the General Sherman Tree is the most massive in the world. It is located in Sequoia National Park, California, U.S.A., and is classified as a giant sequoia. The cubic volume of its trunk is 1,487m^3. We can safely say that this is the largest living organism on earth. It is 83.8 meters tall and is 2,200 years old.

Thirdly, the tallest tree in the world is a redwood called Hyperion, which eclipses the General Sherman Tree in height. Hyperion is 115.55 meters tall, located in Redwood National Park, California. It is about 600 to 800 years old.

Fourthly, the oldest tree on earth is the Bristlecone Pine, which lives in a harsh environment 3,300 meters above sea level. It is approximately 4,700 plus years old. This tree survives in the eastern part of California, but the specific location is kept secret. Therefore, it is not open to public viewing.

Lastly, the widest tree on earth is the Tule Cypress, which stands southwest of Mexico City, Mexico. It is 42 meters tall, 2,000 years old and 14.85 meters wide at the base of the trunk. Although it is but one tree, it appears as a forest when seen from a distance.

In conclusion, we can say trees are the largest and most long-lived life forms in the world. Such are the things forests are made of and forests play an immeasurably beneficial role for human beings. Forests not only produce wood as a resource but provide clean air and clear water. For instance, the costs to create the same amount of clean air and pure water that forests produce in a year are about 1 trillion yen and 15 trillion yen respectively. Since forests are so important to our ecosystem, we should make efforts to protect them.

Naturally, we should also strive to learn more about the trees that make up forests. The more we learn about them, the more important we realize they are and the better we can care for them.

NOTES

dragon's blood tree 竜血樹 / **extraordinary** 並外れた / **blood red** 血のように赤い(blood-redとも表記) / **sap** 樹液 / **Socotra Island** ソコトラ島 / **Yemen** イエメン(アラビア半島最南端に位置する国) / **dyestuff** 染料 / **be characterized by ~** ~を特徴とする / **General Sherman Tree** シャーマン将軍の木 / **Sequoia National Park** セコイア国立公園 / **sequoia** セコイア(スギ科の木) / **cubic volume** 体積 / **organism** 生物 / **redwood** レッドウッド(＝セコイア) / **eclipse ~ in ...** …の点で~をしのぐ / **Redwood National Park** レッドウッド国立公園 / **Bristlecone Pine** ブリスルコーン・パイン / **harsh environment** 過酷な環境 / **Tule Cypress** トゥーレ・サイプレス / **life form** 生命体 / **immeasurably** 計り知れないほどに

COMPREHENSION

次の英文が本文の内容と一致する場合はT、一致しない場合はFを記入しましょう。

1. (　) The sap of the dragon's blood tree is red.
2. (　) The General Sherman Tree is the tallest in the world.
3. (　) The oldest tree in the world is readily accessible for viewing.
4. (　) The widest tree in the world is located in Mexico.
5. (　) It costs about one trillion yen to produce the same amount of pure water that forests provide us in a year.

GRAMMAR

次の英文の空所に入れるのに正しい語句を (A) ～ (D) から選びましょう。

1. The price of the PC I want most is (　　) than any other in the shop, so I can't afford to buy it.
   (A) high　　(B) higher　　(C) the highest　　(D) more high

2. My English teacher's way of teaching had the (　　) effect on the improvement of my English, so even now I am thankful.
   (A) high　　(B) best　　(C) well　　(D) least

3. The old man said to me "Time is (　　) precious thing of all. There's so much I'd still like to do if I were twenty years younger."
   (A) more　　(B) most　　(C) the more　　(D) the most

4. The older I grow, (　　) I realize that things I dismissed as unimportant in the past are actually very important.
   (A) more　　(B) the more　　(C) the most　　(D) as

5. Although I lost the watch that my mother gave to me as a gift, she gently reminded me, "You'll find it when (　　) expected."
   (A) best　　(B) worst　　(C) least　　(D) first

＜文法を理解する＞　11. 最上級同等表現

最上級で表す内容を原級や比較級で表すことができます。以下の例文で確認してみましょう。

「経験ほど貴重なものはありません」

Experience is the most precious thing of all.　　［最上級］
= Nothing is as precious as experience.　　［原級］
= There is nothing as precious as experience.　　［原級］
= Nothing is more precious than experience.　　［比較級］
= There is nothing more precious than experience.　　［比較級］
= Experience is more precious than anything else.　　［比較級］

上記の英文は使われている比較表現は異なっても、表している内容は同じです。原級や比較級でも、自由自在に最上級の内容を表せるようにしましょう。

COMPOSITION

次の英文の(　　)内の単語を並べ換えて、意味の通る文にしましょう。

1. There are many unique animals (in / to / be / deserve / seen / that) Australia.
   (　　　　　　　　　　　　　　　　　　　　　　　　　　　　　　　　　　)

2. We (say / Japan / safely / is / that / can) blessed with many scenic spots and places of historical interest.
   (　　　　　　　　　　　　　　　　　　　　　　　　　　　　　　　　　　)

3. A Portuguese man-of-war called Katsuono Eboshi (but / seems / one / to / body / be); however, it consists of a number of polyps called Hidoro-chu.
   (　　　　　　　　　　　　　　　　　　　　　　　　　　　　　　　　　　)

4. The shape of Gunma Prefecture looks like a flying (when / crane / on / seen / map / a) of all 47 Japanese prefectures.
   (　　　　　　　　　　　　　　　　　　　　　　　　　　　　　　　　　　)

5. Insects' feelers play (in / role / sensing / important / the / an) smell of their females; for example, a male moth can pick up the scent of a female moth a kilometer away.
   (　　　　　　　　　　　　　　　　　　　　　　　　　　　　　　　　　　)

★英語表現の小箱11★　「努力する」の英語

本文でstrive（努力する)が出てきましたが、「努力する」を意味する英語表現も豊富にあります。重要なものをいつか挙げておきましょう。

- 1語⇒ strive; endeavor
- 2語⇒ work hard; try hard; exert oneself
- 3語⇒ make an effort; make an endeavor
- 4語⇒ put forth an effort

参考：take great painsは「大いに努力する」のニュアンス。
　　　また、口語ではplug away at…の言い回しがあります。

Chapter 11 – *Trees of Greatness and the Greatness of Trees*

LISTENING & DICTATION

CD 2-3

次の会話を聞いて、空所に単語を埋めましょう。

A: Do you know what the largest living (1.   ) on earth is? And how about the longest living creature?

B: The (2.   ) whale has got to be the largest. I think the elephant tortoise lives the longest. So, am I right?

A: Not exactly. The blue whale is the largest in the animal kingdom. Blue whales as long as 34 meters have been (3.   ) in the past. The elephant tortoise does live a long time. One has even been (4.   ) for 250 years. But we can (5.   ) say that when considering all life including plants, the answer is a tree.

B: I see. We're talking about all living things then, not just animals. In that case, I heard a tree called a sequoia (6.   ) great heights. The tallest one is about 124 meters high.

A: And among trees dating back to the Jomon period is one that is 7,000 years old. By the way, it is said that Europe has a stone culture, while Japan has a (7.   ) culture. Wood plays a (8.   ) role in Japanese culture. Horyuji is a famous example.

B: Horyuji Temple is the oldest (9.   ) wooden structure in the world, isn't it?

A: Yes. Horyuji is about 1,300 years old, and the Japanese cypress of which Horyuji is made is another 1,000 years older still.

B: Considering the fact that ferroconcrete buildings may (10.   ) only 100 years, the Japanese cypress is a marvelous material indeed.

TIPS 科学よもやま話11　木の不思議

　ペルシャ湾西部に位置するバーレーンで植物が生えない不毛の砂漠にたった1本だけ木が生えています。この木は「生命の木」(tree of life) と呼ばれています。この樹木は、年間150ミリ程度の少ない降水量でも繁茂するようです。また、この木は地中深く50メートルまで根を伸ばし、水を吸収すると考えられています。マメ科アカシア属とみられるこの木は、冬には葉を落としますが、春と秋に黄色い花を咲かせます。地元の人たちは、この木の生えている場所は、聖書に現れる「エデンの園」と考えています。世界遺産に登録され、観光客は毎年5万人に上るようです。

CHAPTER 12

Living Fossils

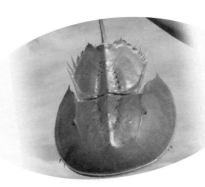

「生きた化石」には5つの区分がありますが、それはどのようなものでしょうか。ムカシトカゲを例に考えてみましょう。また、カブトガニの血液は青色ですが、ヒトに大きく貢献しています。どのように役立っているのでしょうか。

◀ VOCABULARY CHECK ▶

次の単語について、その定義を選び結びつけましょう。

1. resemble ・   ・ (A) to meet certain conditions
2. inherit ・   ・ (B) seeing something that is not readily apparent
3. satisfy ・   ・ (C) liquid that carries oxygen through bodies
4. blood ・   ・ (D) to receive something from someone when they die
5. detection ・ ・ (E) to look like or be similar to another person or thing

PASSAGE

CD 2-4

An organism that thrived in many places in the past but now is rarely seen is called a "relict." A relict continues to closely resemble the shape or nature of its earlier species. Due to this, they are often called living fossils. Living fossils fall into some or all of the following five categories:

(1) Quantity: an organism that once thrived but is now very small in number
(2) Area: an organism that was widespread but now lives in limited areas
(3) Traits: an organism that did not change so much in shape or characteristics
(4) Class: an organism that had many related species in the same group
(5) Environment: an organism that has inherited characteristics suitable to the environment of the remote past

There are very few organisms that satisfy all the above five requirements. In many cases, living fossils satisfy only some of the above. For example, a

Chapter 12 – *Living Fossils*

tuatara, a type of primitive lizard, looks like a closely related species that lived 200 million years ago. It had many related species in the past but now remains as only one species belonging to one group called an "order." Moreover, this species' habitat is limited to only some islands around the North Island of New Zealand. Therefore, this animal meets three of the above requirements.

There are actually quite a few other examples of living fossils. There are Japanese giant salamanders, coelacanths, duckbills, and cockroaches in the animal kingdom and metasequoias, sago cycads, ginkgo trees, and maple trees in the plant kingdom. Among the most famous living fossils is the horseshoe crab.

A horseshoe crab is an arthropod with a body like a soldier's helmet and a tail like a large thorn. Besides being a living fossil, this crab is noteworthy because of its blood. We human beings can benefit greatly from its blood. Its blood is blue and has amoeba-like cells. These cells function to surround bacteria entering the human body, solidifying them. It can also be utilized for early detection of cancer. On top of that, its blood is also used in the examination of water or food. There are great expectations regarding future research into the numerous benefits of the blood of horseshoe crabs.

NOTES

living fossil 生きた化石(「生きている化石」とも) / **organism** 生物 / **thrive** 栄える / **relict** 残存種(「遺存種」とも) / **fall into ~** ~に該当する / **trait** 特徴 / **characteristic** 特性 / **inherit** 受け継ぐ / **remote past** 大昔 / **tuatara** ムカシトカゲ / **primitive** 原始的な / **order** 目[もく](生物分類上の一段階、上位からドメイン、界、門、綱、目、科、属、種の8段階) / **habitat** 生息地 / **quite a few** かなり多くの(＝not a few, a good few) / **Japanese giant salamander** オオサンショウウオ / **coelacanth** シーラカンス / **duckbill** カモノハシ / **cockroach** ゴキブリ / **metasequoia** メタセコイア / **sago cycad** ソテツ / **ginkgo tree** イチョウ / **maple tree** カエデ / **horseshoe crab** カブトガニ / **arthropod** 節足動物 / **thorn** とげ / **amoeba-like** アメーバ状の / **bacteria** 細菌(これは複数形。単数形はbacterium) / **solidify** 固まらせる

COMPREHENSION

次の英文が本文の内容と一致する場合はT、一致しない場合はFを記入しましょう。

1. (　) In order to be regarded as a relict, an organism must have once prospered but now must be very small in number.
2. (　) Today, tuataras thrive in many parts of the world.
3. (　) Duckbills and ginkgo trees are among some examples of living fossils.
4. (　) The blood of a horseshoe crab contains amoeba-like cells.
5. (　) The blood of a horseshoe crab is only useful for the examination of water.

GRAMMAR

次の英文の空所に入れるのに正しい語句を(A)～(D)から選びましょう。

1. (　　　) Ms. Maeda, I met her for the first time in three years yesterday.

    (A) Speak with　(B) Speaking of　(C) To speak　(D) To speak about

2. (　　　) you condemn your parents, put yourself in their place.

    (A) Before　(B) Because　(C) Unless　(D) Until

3. According (　　　) the weather forecast, it will rain tomorrow.

    (A) to　(B) of　(C) for　(D) with

4. Unfortunately, I am no (　　　) at remembering things than Jack.

    (A) better　(B) longer　(C) more　(D) sooner

5. My boss would have given anything for that kind of thing not to (　　　).

    (A) some extent　　　　(B) his heart's content

    (C) tell the truth　　　　(D) have happened

<文法を理解する>　12. 英語の曖昧性Ⅰ

次の英文について考えてみましょう。

　　John walked to the hill in the park.

上記の英文を何と訳しますか。実は、この英文は4通りに和訳することができます。

(1) in the parkが副詞句

…in the parkを副詞句と考えた場合、in the parkはwalkedを修飾することになります。すると、the hillは公園の中にあるのか外にあるのかが不明となります。従って、「ジョンは公園の中を（公園の中にある）丘に向かって歩いた」という和訳と「ジョンは公園の中を（公園の外にある）丘に向かって歩いた」という和訳が成立することになります。

(2) in the parkが形容詞句

…in the parkを形容詞句と考えた場合、in the parkはthe hillを修飾することになります。すると、Johnは公園の中を歩いたのか外を歩いたのかが不明となります。従って、「ジョンは（公園の中を）公園の中にある丘に向かって歩いた」という和訳と「ジョンは（公園の外を）公園の中にある丘に向かって歩いた」という和訳が成立することになります。

Chapter 12 – *Living Fossils*

✏ COMPOSITION

次の英文の（　　　）内の単語を並べ換えて、意味の通る文にしましょう。

1. A living creature called the Ojisan in Japanese (the / of / falls / category / fish / into); the English name for it is the manybar goatfish.
   (   )

2. The Japanese giant salamander's habitat is (of / the / to / upper / limited / waters) a river located only in Japan.
   (   )

3. A mouse is a mammal that can give (to / a / babies / quite / few / birth) in one litter; to be more specific, 6 to 8 babies are born from a mouse at one time.
   (   )

4. The scientist wanted to find support for his hypothesis, though he did not (he / papers / the / all / from / benefit) read so far.
   (   )

5. There are so many things we do not know about our brains; therefore, future (mechanisms / the / of / into / the / research) human brain is to be expected.
   (   )

★英語表現の小箱１２★　「栄える」の英語

本文でthrive（栄える）が出てきました。他にどんな表現があるか挙げてみましょう。
　prosper
　　→ Kamaishi prospered as a steel town.
　　　（釜石は鉄の町として栄えた）
　flourish
　　→ The Sui Dynasty was flourishing in China at that time.
　　　（当時中国では隋王朝が栄えていた）
　参考：The store is prosperous.（その店は栄えている）

LISTENING & DICTATION

次の会話を聞いて、空所に単語を埋めましょう。

A: Dinosaurs (1.   ) the earth over 65 million years ago. Quite a long time before the first humans.

B: Where on (2.   ) did the dinosaurs live?

A: They roamed the entire earth, even what is now Antarctica.

B: But they died out so suddenly. What was the cause?

A: There are various theories regarding that, but among the most (3.   ) is a catastrophic event caused by a meteor. A massive meteorite (4.   ) with the earth sending up fine soil particles from the impact site which entered the atmosphere and covered the earth. This in (5.   ) plunged the earth into a ten-year winter. Due to a lack of food during this ordeal, they went extinct. Other possible causes include flooding and acid rain. Basically dinosaurs were not at all (6.   ) to the changing environment.

B: So only those species that meet the requirements necessary for (7.   ) can survive. Survival of the fittest and all that, huh? By the way, dinosaurs are classified under reptiles, right?

A: That's really not so clear. Some scientists (8.   ) that they not be grouped under the classification of reptile, so they established a new independent (9.   ) for dinosaurs, under which a sub-class of birds exists.

B: In other words, at least some of the dinosaurs (10.   ) into birds, right?

A: That's right. The feathers covering some of the smaller dinosaurs functioned as a means to protect against cold weather, so these survived. After some time, these dinosaurs developed feathered wings and could fly, becoming birds.

TIPS 科学よもやま話１２　青い血

　動物の血は全て赤いとは限りません。エビやカニなどの節足動物、イカやタコまた貝などの軟体動物の血は、一般的に青です。ただし、軟体動物の赤貝や環形動物のゴカイなどは、ヘモグロビンと似た鉄由来のエリトロクルオリンという色素のため、赤い血を持っています。

　青い血の正体は、銅由来のヘモシアニンです。ヘモシアニンは、ヘモグロビンと同じく酸素を運搬する役割を持っていますが、ヘモグロビンとは異なり、血球中に含まれるのではなく、血リンパ液に溶け込んでいます。ヘモシアニン自体は無色ですが、酸素と結び付くことで青色に変化します。

CHAPTER 13

Electric Cars VS Hydrogen Cars

理想の車とは孫悟空の「キン斗雲」なのだとか。「キン斗雲」の何が素晴らしいのでしょうか。また、ガソリン車に代わって期待される電気自動車と水素自動車の長所と短所は何でしょうか。

◀ VOCABULARY CHECK ▶

次の単語について、その定義を選び結びつけましょう。

1. executive・   ・(A) something that happens or exists
2. storage・   ・(B) the space where things can be kept
3. electricity・ ・(C) a position of considerable power in a company
4. emission・   ・(D) the production or giving off of light, heat, gas, etc.
5. occurrence・   ・(E) a form of energy from charged elementary particles

📝 PASSAGE

CD 2-6

   According to Mr. Tatehito Ueda, president of Taiho Kogyo Co. Ltd., the ideal vehicle is the magical Kintoun Cloud of the Monkey King (Sun Wukong). It's made up solely of water vapor, which is 100 percent recyclable and practically non-material. The energy source is will power (psychokinesis), so there is no need for a fuel supply and the inevitable exhaust of CO_2. Moreover, driving is 5 done through one's consciousness alone; therefore, there is little danger of its pilot losing control or colliding with anything since they instinctually don't want to crash.

   Toward this ideal concept, the first thing to solve is finding a new energy source. At present, we rely mostly on gasoline which allows for engines that 10 produce more horsepower than those of electric cars. A car running on gasoline can also takes up less space than what a hydrogen car requires due to the space needed for the storage of hydrogen gas.

   But while gasoline-operated vehicles have merits, there are also significant demerits. Gasoline, which is the generic name for oil products with a boiling 15 point between 30 to 220 degrees Celsius, comes from a limited resource, oil.

Moreover, it pollutes the air with CO_2, NOx and SOx when burned. That's why these days electricity is seen as a viable alternative energy candidate.

An electrically-powered vehicle has a number of advantages, such as being eco-friendly, as it doesn't discharge exhaust fumes, being free from vibration or noise, as well as being fuel-efficient. However, besides the lack of horsepower mentioned earlier, this technology is costly and the engine takes time to charge. Moreover, few charging stations are available. Furthermore, its battery's life is short.

Among other possibilities attracting our attention is the hydrogen vehicle. The hydrogen car is an automobile that uses hydrogen as fuel. Energy is produced by the reaction of hydrogen and oxygen, resulting in the production of water, a clean emission. The energy creating process is in fact the opposite of the electrolysis of water, or the breaking down of water into hydrogen and oxygen molecules.

The problems with hydrogen vehicles include the method of transferring vast amounts of hydrogen into the car, the frequent occurrence of knocking or backfiring and the production of nitrogen oxides created during the process of high-temperature combustion.

NOTES

Monkey King 孫悟空（＝Sun Wukong）/ **water vapor** 水蒸気 / **recyclable** リサイクルできる / **practically** ほとんど / **non-material** 非物質的な / **psychokinesis** 念力 / **inevitable** 不可避の / **exhaust** 排出 / **collide with ～** ～と衝突する / **instinctually** 本能的に / **horsepower** 馬力 / **hydrogen car** 水素自動車 / **generic name** 総称 / **boiling point** 沸点 / **degree Celsius** セ氏温度 / **pollute** 汚染する / **NOx** 窒素酸化物（＝ nitrogen oxides）/ **SOx** 硫黄酸化物（＝ sulfur oxides）/ **viable** 実行可能な / **eco-friendly** 環境に優しい / **discharge** 排出する / **exhaust fume** 排ガス / **fuel-efficient** 低燃費の / **charging station** 充電所 / **electrolysis** 電気分解 / **molecule** 分子 / **combustion** 燃焼

COMPREHENSION

次の英文が本文の内容と一致する場合はT、一致しない場合はFを記入しましょう。

1. (　)　The reason why the Kintoun Cloud is an ideal vehicle is that it gives off CO_2 emissions.
2. (　)　At present, most cars run on gasoline.
3. (　)　Electric cars do not produce exhaust gas.
4. (　)　Hydrogen cars produce energy through the reaction of hydrogen and oxygen.
5. (　)　The sole problem of hydrogen cars is the large space needed for hydrogen.

Chapter 13 – *Electric Cars VS Hydrogen Cars*

GRAMMAR

次の英文の空所に入れるのに正しい語句を (A) ～ (D) から選びましょう。

1. We know a man (　　　) first and last names are the same as our professor's.
   (A) who　　　(B) whom　　　(C) which　　　(D) whose

2. Don't forget (　　　) your friend has just told you. I think it'll be important when you start looking for a job.
   (A) that　　　(B) which　　　(C) what　　　(D) as

3. The reason (　　　) I didn't send out an invitation to you was simply because I didn't know your address.
   (A) which　　　(B) why　　　(C) what　　　(D) how

4. My dream is to get rich and live in a castle (　　　) there are many rooms full of beautiful furniture.
   (A) which　　　(B) of where　　　(C) in which　　　(D) of which

5. (　　　) appears from this paper, she is well versed in the Theory of Relativity.
   (A) As　　　(B) Since　　　(C) That　　　(D) Which

＜文法を理解する＞　13. 完全文か不完全文か

次の問題を考えてみましょう。
　　This is the place (　　　) I lived in two years ago.
　　(A) which　　(B) where

選択肢 (A) の which は関係代名詞、選択肢 (B) の where は関係副詞です。そして、先行詞が the place です。この問題を先行詞が場所を表しているので、(B) の where が正解だと考えていませんか。英文をよく見ると、空所の後の in の直後に本来であれば前置詞の目的語となるべき名詞がありません。つまり、空所の後は不完全文になっています。従って、正解は (A) の which となります。このように、関係代名詞か関係副詞かの区別は、後続する文が不完全文であれば関係代名詞、完全文であれば関係副詞となることに注意しましょう。このことをまとめると、次のようになります。

関係代名詞 (who / whom / which / whose / that) ＋不完全文
関係副詞 (when / where / why) ＋完全文
注：関係副詞 how には先行詞は付かない (＝ the way how はない)。

先行詞

63

✎ COMPOSITION

次の英文の(　　　)内の単語を並べ換えて、意味の通る文にしましょう。

1. There must be rogue software on the computer, since its ad often warns us that (system / danger / crashing / of / in / is / our).
   (　　　　　　　　　　　　　　　　　　　　　　　　　　　　　　　　　　　　)

2. (for / do / thing / to / first / us / the) to solve global warming is to try not to use air conditioners frequently.
   (　　　　　　　　　　　　　　　　　　　　　　　　　　　　　　　　　　　　)

3. People (on / much / rely / too / to / tend / smartphones) in life and on computers at work.
   (　　　　　　　　　　　　　　　　　　　　　　　　　　　　　　　　　　　　)

4. Nobody is (falling / free / of / from / into / danger / the) lifestyle-related diseases when they get older, and especially, fatter.
   (　　　　　　　　　　　　　　　　　　　　　　　　　　　　　　　　　　　　)

5. It (PC / usually / a / takes / restore / time / to) with CPU problems; it is often better to just buy another PC, since new PCs are cheap and perform well.
   (　　　　　　　　　　　　　　　　　　　　　　　　　　　　　　　　　　　　)

★英語表現の小箱１３★　electricityの関連語

本文ではelectricity（電気）という単語が出てきましたが、次の単語の関係に注意しましょう。

	電気	電子
名詞	electricity（電気）	electron（電子）
形容詞	electric（電気の）	electronic（電子の）

注：electric（形容詞）からelectricity（名詞）が派生しているのに対し、electron（名詞）からelectronic（形容詞）が派生しています。

参考：protonは「陽子」、neutronは「中性子」、meson[=mesotron]は「中間子」

Chapter 13 – *Electric Cars VS Hydrogen Cars*

LISTENING & DICTATION

次の会話を聞いて、空所に単語を埋めましょう。

A: An electric car is environmentally friendly mostly because it does not (1.   ) off CO_2 or NOx emissions, which are harmful to the environment, as you know. But there are many other advantages.

B: What kind of advantages?

A: Compared with (2.   ) combustion engines, energy efficiency is very high, (3.   ) in lower energy costs. Utilizing electrical power (4.   ) for a cost of only one yen per kilometer of driving. In the case of gasoline, about 15 yen is needed for each kilometer on the road.

B: Tell me about it. It (5.   ) me an arm and a leg every week.

A: Moreover, idling isn't a problem. When stopping temporarily, the car doesn't wastefully (6.   ) energy.

B: There's got to be some (7.   ). I would guess a machine like this would be overly complicated and difficult to service.

A: It's actually not so complicated. Compared to cars that run on gasoline, there are far fewer parts used in electric cars. When (8.   ), the cars will not require huge (9.   ) of money for repairs. The only real complications arise from the electrical charging systems.

B: I see. Even though they aren't perfect, electric cars will surely be more prevalent in the near future due to all the (10.   ) aspects.

TIPS 科学よもやま話13　電気自動車の弱点

- 交流100ボルトで充電する場合、充電完了まで約14時間必要。
- 電池が高価で、20kWh電池で80万円。
- 充電スタンドが商業として成立しておらず、各社の対応もバラバラ。
- ヒーターに内燃機関の廃熱が使えないので、暖房使用時に航続距離（＝1回の燃料によって走行できる距離）が短くなる。

　しかし、環境に優しくエネルギー効率も高く、しかも、部品点数も比較的少ないので修理コストも抑えられる電気自動車は、将来の自動車の主流になる可能性が高いと思われます。

CHAPTER 14

The Future of Smartphones

携帯電話が普及してしばらく経ち、最近ではスマートフォンを使っている人が増えています。スマートフォンは今までの携帯電話と何が違うのでしょうか。また将来的には、どのように進化していくのでしょうか。

◀ VOCABULARY CHECK ▶

次の単語について、その定義を選び結びつけましょう。

1. house・ ・(A) to open a computer file or gain entry to something
2. represent・ ・(B) to be a symbol of something
3. access・ ・(C) to provide a place for something to be kept
4. pinpoint・ ・(D) to show the exact position of something or someone
5. incorporate・ ・(E) to include something so that it forms a part of another

PASSAGE

The word "smartphone" refers to a form of mobile phone which in Japan is known as "sumaho." Therefore, an interesting new phrase "sumaho walking," which means walking while using a smartphone, came into being.

Smartphones are not merely mobile phones. They house many applications, and among the most noteworthy are the PC-like functions represented by document preparation tools through PDF, Word or Excel, as well as Internet access and e-mailing.

They connect to the Internet through Wi-Fi access, one of the standards of wireless LAN (local area network), and often come with a personal hotspot function that enables other nearby computers and phones to access the Internet.

Smartphones with a Global Positioning System, or GPS, function are also available. GPS is used to identify the present geographical location of electronic devices. Information from several satellites from among the 30-odd military-based satellites launched by the U.S. is received by GPS receptors to pinpoint a present position. Errors of just one millionth of a second can result in a difference of 300 meters in distance; therefore, data collected from four satellites is necessary in order to calculate a precise location. GPS has previously been in use in car navigation devices, and the installment of a GPS function into smartphones allows phones to be used as a portable car navigation system.

As a result, smartphones are not mere phones. They are chock-full of an abundance of useful functions.

While smartphones are very convenient as is, in the not-too-distant future they may be worn as we do an article of clothing such as a watch or bracelet. Or they may even be incorporated into our clothes. If a smartphone is part of our garment, there will be no danger of dropping or leaving it somewhere.

Improved voice recognition software will allow accurate e-mails to be produced simply by uttering what you want to say into the device. It is expected that even though a plethora of new functions will be introduced, smartphones will continue to increase in ease of use. It is a total mystery as to what the world will be like 20 years from now, just as we did not expect today's development of mobile phones 20 years ago. There is no telling what will happen in the future; it may be a world beyond imagination!

NOTES

mobile phone 携帯電話 / **come into being** 生じる / **merely** 単に / **house** 内蔵する / **document preparation tool** 文書作成ツール / **personal hotspot function** テザリング機能 / **Global Positioning System** 全地球測位網 / **identify** 特定する / **geographical** 地理的な / **electronic device** 電子機器 / **satellite** 衛星 / **from among ~** ~の中から / **~-odd** ~余りの / **receptor** 受信機 / **error** 誤差 / **one millionth of a second** 100万分の1秒 / **calculate** 算出する / **previously** 以前は / **installment** 取り付け / **chock-full** ぎっしり詰まった(アメリカ英語の口語表現) / **an abundance of ~** 豊富な~ / **as is** 現状で / **not-too-distant future** そう遠くはない将来 / **article of clothing** 衣料品 / **garment** 衣服 / **a plethora of ~** 過度の~

COMPREHENSION

次の英文が本文の内容と一致する場合はT、一致しない場合はFを記入しましょう。

1. (　) Smartphones have some of the same functions as personal computers.
2. (　) Smartphones with tethering functions have not yet been developed.
3. (　) Some smartphones contain GPS functions.
4. (　) At present smartphones have already been integrated into our clothing.
5. (　) It is quite easy to predict what will happen 20 years from now.

GRAMMAR

次の英文の空所に入れるのに正しい語句を(A)〜(D)から選びましょう。

1. The gentleman bought all the (   ) boxes at my store, which made me very happy.

    (A) little ten blue wooden (B) ten little blue wooden
    (C) ten wooden little blue (D) ten little wooden blue

2. Ellie works hard in the office for a (   ) salary without making so much as a peep regarding how unfairly she is treated.

    (A) little   (B) few   (C) less   (D) small

3. It was (   ) of him to reject the job offer because the company went bankrupt.

    (A) sensitive   (B) sensible   (C) sensory   (D) sensuous

4. You should be (   ) your parents whether you like them or not.

    (A) respect   (B) respectful   (C) respectable   (D) respectful to

5. My grandmother is looked up to by her neighbors since she knows much about traditional Japanese (   ) events.

    (A) ceremony   (B) ceremonious   (C) ceremonial   (D) ceremoniously

<文法を理解する> 14. 形容詞の語順

前置修飾の形容詞を並べる際、次のようなルールがあります。

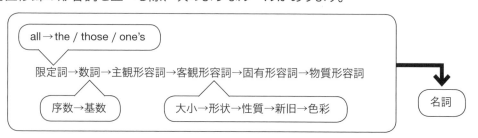

なお、同じ種類(＝レベル)の形容詞はコンマまたはandを用いて表現するのが普通です。このルールは形容詞のレベルが違うと当てはまりません。

○ John is a big, tall boy. / ○ John is a big and tall boy.
　　注：bigとtallは大小に関する形容詞
× This is a big, wooden box. / × This is a big and wooden box.

Chapter 14 – *The Future of Smartphones*

COMPOSITION

次の英文の(　　)内の単語を並べ換えて、意味の通る文にしましょう。

1. A group of the world's top physicists finally found the very (came / moment / universe / being / when / into / the).
   (　　　　　　　　　　　　　　　　　　　　　　　　　　　　　　　)

2. Litmus (check / paper / whether / used / usually / is / to) a water solution is acidic or alkaline.
   (　　　　　　　　　　　　　　　　　　　　　　　　　　　　　　　)

3. Multiple functions of a smartphone (us / allow / an / like / to / things / use) alarm, a calculator, a calendar, a camera, a recording machine, a game console and many others.
   (　　　　　　　　　　　　　　　　　　　　　　　　　　　　　　　)

4. We cannot say that if there are no volcanoes nearby, there is (of / large / occurring / no / earthquake / any / danger) in the near future.
   (　　　　　　　　　　　　　　　　　　　　　　　　　　　　　　　)

5. I would like to do some specific research (be / can / as / what / found / relationship / to) between people's favorite colors and their personality.
   (　　　　　　　　　　　　　　　　　　　　　　　　　　　　　　　)

★英語表現の小箱１４★　名詞で有名な動詞

本文ではhouse（〜を収容する，〜を内蔵する）が出てきましたが、英語では名詞で有名な単語が動詞でも使用されることがよくあります。いくつか挙げてみましょう。

　　She watered the flowers.（彼女は花に水をやった）
　　He aired his jacket out in the park.（彼は公園で上着を［風に当てて］乾かした）
　　The story fired the girl's imagination.
　　（その話はその少女の想像力をかきたてた）

LISTENING & DICTATION

次の会話を聞いて、空所に単語を埋めましょう。

A: It's unbelievable how TVs have morphed into flat screens and phones have been (1.   ) by smartphones. It's noteworthy that 20 years ago few could (2.   ) exactly how much technology would change. There is no knowing what the world 20 years from now will look like. What do you think will be the state of things years from now?

B: I'm (3.   ) smartphones will be incorporated into watches or glasses, and when you need to e-mail someone or (4.   ) the net, you'll be able to project a virtual display at your convenience. Your desk could immediately become a display on which you can enjoy computer games.

A: I think highly (5.   ) simultaneous translating software will be around. If you ask a question to an English-speaking person in Japanese, they will be able to hear the translation fed directly to their (6.   ) through an earphone. This kind of software would (7.   ) the person's English answer to be quickly translated into Japanese, and then understood through your own earphone.

B: If that system (8.   ) out to be accurate enough, there will be little use for English teachers in 20 years.

A: English teachers may (9.   ) up teaching mostly those who want to learn the language as a hobby.

B: I'm really looking (10.   ) to seeing what will happen down the road.

TIPS 科学よもやま話14　スマホの驚くべきアプリ

スマホでできる驚きのアプリを挙げてみましょう。
1. カメラで写した言葉をリアルタイムに翻訳できる。
2. 写真を撮るだけで被写体の寸法が測れる。
3. ビデオを撮るだけで、早送り動画の作成が可能。
4. 町で聞こえた音楽を聞かせると、曲名を言ってくれる。
5. 夜空に向けると、その方向にある星座を教えてくれる。
6. 名刺の情報が自動でインプットされる。
7. 誕生会のろうそくの火を消せる。

最後のアプリの仕組みは単純です。スピーカーから風が出る仕組みになっているのです。

CHAPTER 15
Technology Learned from Animals

動物はすごい能力を持っています。科学技術のさまざまな分野で、その動物の能力が活用されています。どんな動物の、どのような能力が科学技術に応用されているのでしょうか。

◀ VOCABULARY CHECK ▶

次の単語について、その定義を選び結びつけましょう。

1. invent • • (A) to puncture or go through something
2. explore • • (B) to inquire into or discuss something in detail
3. manage • • (C) to imitate someone or something in action or appearance
4. mimic • • (D) to create something that has not existed before
5. pierce • • (E) to succeed in achieving something difficult

PASSAGE

CD 2-10

 The Wright brothers, famous for inventing the airplane, are said to have studied the way a bird flies and incorporated what they learned into the design of their planes. They had discovered the fact that the upper surface and lower surface of a bird's wings are curved differently.

 A spider's thread looks fragile but according to recent research, it is 10 times as strong as steel if they were the same weight. Ongoing research is exploring the mechanism of the spider's organs in which such a durable thread is made under normal temperature and pressure without drawing on too much energy.

 We can safely say that animals that manage to survive in hazardous environments have acquired the means to do so through the enormous time span of 3.8 billion years. From such animals we can learn a lot; in fact, some of what we learned is now utilized in practical ways.

 Take bullet trains for example. The pointed head of the train mimics the bill of a kingfisher. High pressure due to resistance occurs when the bullet train enters a tunnel, resulting in a tremendously loud roar throughout the tunnel. It was found that to reduce noise, the shape of the kingfisher's bill is most effective. The kingfisher dives into water elegantly with almost no splashing even though the pressure of the bird's mass against the water should be great.

Dubai's high-rise buildings and Zimbabwe's East Gate Center, which do not rely on air-conditioning devices, are modeled after an anthill. Cold air is taken in from a vent and hot air is sent out from a chimney. This design is very economical as its energy consumption is one tenth of a building with typical ventilation and air-conditioning devices.

Prof. Seiji Aoyagi of Kansai University studied the blood-sucking abilities of mosquitoes and was able to invent a hypodermic needle that causes no pain. He learned that a mosquito bite pierces the skin of animals with three needles operated together and applied this to a needle. The width of this new needle is 0.015 mm and the injector consists of three small needles similar to a mosquito's. And like a mosquito, this system seems to contribute to painless injections.

The field of science which produces new technologies by mimicking a living creature's functions is called biomimicry. Further studies are to be expected in this area of research.

NOTES

fragile もろい / **durable** 丈夫な / **mimic** 模倣する / **bill** 嘴［くちばし］/ **kingfisher** カワセミ（ブッポウソウ目の鳥）/ **Dubai** ドバイ（アラブ首長国連邦を構成する首長国の1つ）/ **Zimbabwe** ジンバブエ（アフリカ大陸南部の内陸国）/ **anthill** アリ塚 / **hypodermic** 皮下の / **needle** 注射針 / **injector** 注射器 / **mimicking** : mimicのing形（cで終わる動詞のingにはkを付ける→picnicking）/ **biomimicry** バイオミミクリー（生物模倣）

COMPREHENSION

次の英文が本文の内容と一致する場合はT、一致しない場合はFを記入しましょう。

1. (　) The Wright brothers applied the way a bat flies to their design of the airplane.
2. (　) Steel is one tenth of a spider's thread in strength if they weigh the same.
3. (　) In fact, there are very few animals that we can learn a lot from.
4. (　) The pointed head of a bullet train is modeled after a kingfisher's tail.

5. (　) The blood-sucking mechanism of a mosquito was utilized for the air-conditioning devices of high-rise buildings in Dubai.

GRAMMAR

次の英文の空所に入れるのに正しい語句を (A) 〜 (D) から選びましょう。

1. A unicellular animal is said to be representative of a (　　) life form.
   (A) low　　　(B) lower　　　(C) lowest　　　(D) most low

2. An African bush elephant is about (　　) a human being.
   (A) 100 times heavy　　　(B) the weight of 100 times of
   (C) 100 times more weight than　　　(D) 100 times as heavy as

3. The zoologist's argument about the new species was (　　) convincing.
   (A) greater　　　(B) such　　　(C) most　　　(D) well

4. The life span of a wild giraffe is about (　　) of that of a human being.
   (A) one six　　　(B) one sixth　　　(C) first six　　　(D) one of six

5. There is every reason to expect that (　　) research about animals will help promote science and technology for the benefit of us human beings.
   (A) far　　　(B) farther　　　(C) further　　　(D) by far

<文法を理解する>　15. 特殊な比較変化

形容詞や副詞には、比較級と最上級の形があり、元の形を原級と言います。比較級・最上級の変化が、次のように意味によって異なるものがあるので、要注意です。
（1）old ［年老いた］　　　old --- older --- oldest
　　　　　［年上の］　　　　old --- elder --- eldest（限定用法のみ）
（2）late ［（時間が）遅い］　late --- later --- latest
　　　　　［（順序が）後の］　late --- latter --- last
（3）far　［（距離が）遠い］　far --- farther --- farthest
　　　　　［（程度が）さらに］　far --- further --- furthest
注：later は副詞として「後で」、latest は形容詞で「最新の」、latter は「後者の」など独立して使われることが多い。

COMPOSITION

次の英文の(　　　)内の単語を並べ換えて、意味の通る文にしましょう。

1. The special correspondent incorporated the (visited / the / he / information / into / country / about) a long report.
   (　　　　　　　　　　　　　　　　　　　　　　　　　　　　　　　　)

2. Her (a / work / has / profit / resulted / large / in), so everyone around her was a bit jealous of her success.
   (　　　　　　　　　　　　　　　　　　　　　　　　　　　　　　　　)

3. The newly developed automobile (modeled / to / been / after / considered / have / is) the elegant shape of a cheetah.
   (　　　　　　　　　　　　　　　　　　　　　　　　　　　　　　　　)

4. The issue is going to be discussed (consisting / newly / committee / of / at / the / six) elected members tomorrow morning.
   (　　　　　　　　　　　　　　　　　　　　　　　　　　　　　　　　)

5. Now there is a scientist with the potential to (for / to / contribute / great / able / something / be) the world.
   (　　　　　　　　　　　　　　　　　　　　　　　　　　　　　　　　)

★英語表現の小箱15★　複合語＜O+V-ing＞の形

本文でair-conditioning（空調の）やblood-sucking（吸血の）が出てきましたが、これらは、＜目的語＋動詞ing＞の形で形容詞となっている複合形容詞です。いくつか例を挙げておきましょう。

　　plant-eating 草食の　（＝herbivorous）
　　meat-eating 肉食の　（＝carnivorous）
　　fund-raising 資金集めの
　　deficit-covering 赤字を埋め合わせる
　　　※deficit-covering national bondsは「赤字国債」（＝赤字補填［ほてん］のための国債）。

Chapter 15 – *Technology Learned from Animals*

🎧 LISTENING & DICTATION CD 2-11

次の会話を聞いて、空所に単語を埋めましょう。

A: Nancy, did you know that a feature of a certain animal is (1.   ) to be utilized in the design of the pantograph of a bullet train?

B: George, what did you say? You said panto... something? What is that?

A: I said "pantograph." A pantograph is an electric current-(2.   ) device placed on the roof of a train.

B: Oh, I see. So that's what you're talking about. I think I've seen (3.   ) actually. It has some kind of (4.   ) to an animal?

A: Yes, indeed. A (5.   ) one, too. You have one as a pet.

B: What? I (6.   ) a dog. Is it a dog?

A: No, it's a type of bird.

B: Oh, my owl. It's news to me that owls are said to have (7.   ) to the technology in any way. The shape of a part of the pantograph is similar (8.   ) that of an owl's head or something?

A: Well, not quite. You see owls fly very quietly. The secret is their wings' saw-like zigzag patterns, which help them (9.   ) the wind evenly across the surface of their wings. This feature is (10.   ) to the pantograph of trains.

TIPS 科学よもやま話１５　　犬の話

　犬と猫は、人間に好かれているペットの双壁といえるでしょう。その犬は、実はネコ目イヌ科に属しています。

　国際畜犬連盟（FCI）は現在３３１犬種を公認しています。全世界に約４億匹の犬がいると考えられています。血液型は８種類です。

　何といっても、犬は嗅覚が優れています。人間の数千から数万倍の嗅覚能力を持つといわれていますが、酢酸のにおいなどは、人間の一億倍まで感知できるようです。

　しかし犬だけが嗅覚において優れているというわけではありません。熊の嗅覚は犬の約７倍で、象は犬や熊をもはるかにしのぐと考えられています。

　犬にネギを与えてはいけないのは、ネギに含まれる成分（アリルプロピルジスルファイドなど）が犬の赤血球を溶かし、貧血を起こさせるからです。チョコレート、牛乳、アボカド、タケノコなども与えない方がよいとされています。

CHAPTER 16

Rainfall by Laser

自然の恵みの1つ、雨。雨が降らなければ人は生きていけないかもしれません。だから、人は科学の力で雨を降らせようとしています。どのようにしたら雨を降らせることができるのでしょうか。

◀ VOCABULARY CHECK ▶

次の単語について、その定義を選び結びつけましょう。

1. tradition ・   ・ (A) a careful study of a subject
2. weather ・   ・ (B) the condition of the atmosphere
3. air ・   ・ (C) the mixture of gases that we breathe
4. research ・   ・ (D) a state in which opposite influences exist in equal amounts
5. balance ・   ・ (E) a belief or custom that has existed for a long time

PASSAGE

　　In 824, Kukai and Shubin, who regarded Kukai as his rival, performed a rainmaking ritual on the Imperial order of Emperor Junna. According to tradition, Shubin's power caused rain to fall only in Kyoto, but Kukai was able to successfully conjure rain across the whole of Japan for three days. This is
5　one of a number of examples of the act of ritually summoning rain in Japan. Besides Japan, countries from all over the world practice similar kinds of religious ceremonies. By attributing the act of controlling weather to religion and mysticism, it has been a power that is unattainable by ordinary people. This means that only those of high status in their religion are thought to have
10　the power to summon storms.

　　However, in recent years, a series of scientific experiments to cause rainfall through science has met with some success. For example, the Chinese have a method of creating rain artificially through the use of silver iodide.

　　To do this, silver iodide is fired into a cloud by using small rockets. Then
15　particles of snow are formed with silver iodide as their nucleus, which then fall

Chapter 16 – *Rainfall by Laser*

as rain. It is important to note that this chemical substance is considered to be unhealthy and harmful to the environment.

Therefore, a new method of rainmaking using lasers is now being researched. Small particles of nitric acid are produced by the directing of laser beams at moist air. These nitric acid particles function as a vehicle, changing water molecules into water grains. This is regarded as the water-grain producing mechanism.

There are two advantages in laser rainmaking. One is that there is no need to use chemical substances that may affect the environment or human body. The other is that the system is easier to control than when using chemicals.

However, the disadvantage is that it is costly due to the amount of power generating a laser takes. More information is needed on the precise mechanism of rainfall, too. That is, more research is needed on the effect artificial rainmaking has on the environment.

Last but not least, we have to contemplate whether or not we even have the right to manipulate the sky's natural functions as we already do with the earth. The balance between the development of science and technology and the protection of nature is extremely important.

NOTES

Kukai 空海 **Shubin** 守敏（ともに平安時代の僧）/ **rainmaking ritual** 雨乞いの儀式 / **Imperial order** 詔［みことのり］、詔勅［しょうちょく］（直訳は「天皇の命令」、意訳して「詔」・「詔勅」）/ **Emperor Junna** 淳和天皇 / **conjure** 呪文で呼び出す / **ritually** 儀式として / **summon** 呼び起こす / **attribute A to B** AはBに起因すると考える / **mysticism** 神秘主義 / **unattainable** 達成できない / **ordinary people** 一般人，民衆 / **meet with success** 成功する / **artificially** 人工的に / **silver iodide** ヨウ化銀（銀のヨウ化物で、化学式はAgI。人工降雨の際には凍結核として使われる）/ **particle** 粒子 / **nucleus** 中心部分 / **nitric acid** 硝酸（化学式はHNO₃）/ **vehicle** 媒体 / **molecule** 分子 / **grain** 粒 / **precise** 正確な / **last but not least** 大切なことを言い忘れていたが / **contemplate** 熟考する / **manipulate** 操作する / **sky's natural functions** 天候

COMPREHENSION

次の英文が本文の内容と一致する場合はT、一致しない場合はFを記入しましょう。

1. (　) Shubin and Kukai were both successful in causing rain, but only in Kyoto.
2. (　) It is possible to cause rain artificially if we use silver iodine.
3. (　) When we produce artificial rain by using lasers, small nitric acid particles function as a vehicle.
4. (　) One of the advantages in laser-based rainmaking is that it is less costly.
5. (　) We should consider carefully whether humans have the right to control weather.

GRAMMAR

次の英文の空所に入れるのに正しい語句を(A) ～ (D)から選びましょう。

1. The television station decided on a new series (　　　) monthly TV programs so as to stem the overall decline in ratings.

   (A) to　　　　(B) of　　　　(C) for　　　　(D) with

2. The experts worry about harmful effects caused (　　　) the current changes of the earth's environment.

   (A) to　　　　(B) of　　　　(C) in　　　　(D) by

3. The president apologized to people for his improper behavior in the handling (　　　) the incident.

   (A) at　　　　(B) on　　　　(C) in　　　　(D) of

4. Ecologically-friendly cars are not (　　　) to the environment.

   (A) harm　　　(B) harmful　　(C) harmfully　　(D) harmfulness

5. The professor has a habit of sitting in his chair with his legs (　　　).

   (A) cross　　　(B) crossing　　(C) crossed　　(D) to cross

> **<文法を理解する>　16. 可算名詞と不可算名詞**
>
> 名詞を分類する方法として次の2通りがあります。
>
> 　　(1) 可算性の観点：可算名詞、不可算名詞
> 　　(2) 意味や性質の観点：普通名詞、集合名詞、固有名詞、抽象名詞
>
> 特に(1)の観点は重要で、可算名詞(countable noun)と不可算名詞(uncountable noun)の区別は文法問題をはじめ、さまざまなところで問題となってきます。以下が注意すべき不可算名詞のリストです。
>
> advice（忠告）/ baggage（手荷物）/ damage（損害）/ harm（害）/ furniture（家具類）/ homework（宿題）/ housework（家事）/ information（情報）/ luggage（旅行かばん[集合的]）/ machinery（機械類）/ scenery（景色）/ poetry（詩[集合的]）/ mail（郵便物）/ news（知らせ）/ progress（進歩）/ room（余地）/ traffic（交通量）/ weather（天候）/ work（仕事）
>
> 　　注1：assignmentはアメリカ英語で「宿題」という意味の場合、可算名詞です。
> 　　注2：workは「作品」という意味の場合、可算名詞です。

✎ COMPOSITION

次の英文の（　　　）内の単語を並べ換えて、意味の通る文にしましょう。

1. Gunpowder (said / of / sometimes / be / one / is / to) the three major inventions, the others being the compass and the printing press.
   (　　　　　　　　　　　　　　　　　　　　　　　　　　　　　　　)

2. A (geophysics / of / series / on / been / lectures / has) given to students at the university three times by Professor Adams.
   (　　　　　　　　　　　　　　　　　　　　　　　　　　　　　　　)

3. The (the / environment / to / substance / is / chemical / harmful); the important thing is we try to keep the pollution to a minimum.
   (　　　　　　　　　　　　　　　　　　　　　　　　　　　　　　　)

4. There (to / need / for / seemed / researcher / the / no) conduct further experiments; his results had brought a satisfactory solution to the underlying issues.
   (　　　　　　　　　　　　　　　　　　　　　　　　　　　　　　　)

5. Roughly speaking, there are two causes for a hernia of intervertebral disk: One is, as everybody expects, aging; (the / people's / is / lifestyle / to / related / other).
   (　　　　　　　　　　　　　　　　　　　　　　　　　　　　　　　)

★英語表現の小箱１６★　　onlyとaloneの使い方

本文で「〜だけ」を意味するonlyとaloneが出てきていますが、用法は異なるので注意しましょう。

例えば「Xだけ(が)」を意味する時、語順が異なります。つまり、onlyを用いる場合は、only Xというのに対し、aloneはX aloneとします。

　注：onlyと冠詞の位置と意味の違い
　　　an only child（一人っ子）; only a child（ほんの子供[にすぎない]）
　　　the only child（唯一の子）; only the child（その子だけ[が]）

LISTENING & DICTATION

次の会話を聞いて、空所に単語を埋めましょう。

A: I happen to know that some interesting research is being (1.   ) on rainmaking by using laser beams. You have some knowledge of the field of optics, so you should be able to help me get the bigger (2.   ) here. I've seen red or green laser beams used at concerts and such but what other (3.   ) can you think of?

B: Laser printers print documents by utilizing lasers, and disk drives can read the data on CD-ROMs and DVDs through lasers.

A: How can different (4.   ) of laser beams be produced?

B: Different wavelengths (5.   ) colors. Long wavelengths produce red beams, while short ones produce blue.

A: I hear lasers can be used to (6.   ) distances.

B: They can. It's important to (7.   ) that despite interference of natural light, lasers will not diffuse. Therefore, we can measure distance by noting the time it takes for the beam to come back after it hits an (8.   ).

A: Fascinating! How fast is a laser beam?

B: The beam itself is light. So about 300,000 km per (9.   ); it's extraordinarily fast.

A: I guess so! Considering light can go around the earth (10.   ) and a half times in one second.

TIPS 科学よもやま話１６　光についての基礎知識

　光が伝播する速度である「光速度」は宇宙における最大速度です。真空中で毎秒約３０万キロメートルです。正確には、299,792.458 km/sです。この数値、覚え方があります。「憎くなく(29979)、二人(2)寄れば(4)、いつも(5)ハッピー(8)」です。

　光は地球から月まで1.3秒で、地球から太陽まで8分19秒で届きます。そんなとてつもなく速い速度である光速度も、物質中では遅くなり、例えば、水中では秒速約22.5万キロメートルになります。

　光が1年かかって到達する距離を「1光年」といいます。正確に計算すると、9兆4,607億3,047万2,580.800 km です。概数としては、約9.46×10^{15}メートル（約9.46ペタメートル）となります。太陽系から最も近い恒星であるプロキシマ・ケンタウリは太陽から4.22光年、銀河系の直径は約10万光年、隣の銀河であるアンドロメダ銀河までは250万光年、観測可能な宇宙の果てまでは、約465億光年とされています。

CHAPTER 17

The Mystery of the Moon

月は地球の潮の満ち引きに影響を与えていますが、それはどのような影響でしょうか。また、計算上は、たった1枚の紙だけで月に行くことができるのですが、それはどうすればよいのでしょうか。

◀ VOCABULARY CHECK ▶

次の単語について、その定義を選び結びつけましょう。

1. fold   •   • (A) to add a number to itself a particular number of times
2. multiply •   • (B) to bend something over onto itself
3. assume •   • (C) to show something is definitely true or correct
4. contain •   • (D) to have something inside or include something as a part
5. confirm •   • (E) to think something could be true

PASSAGE   CD 2-14

We can reach the moon with one sheet of paper without depending on rocketry. If we fold the paper in half 43 times, the thickness will be about 0.7 million km, which is more than sufficient distance to reach the moon (its distance from the earth is about 0.38 million km). Though this is astonishing, there is mathematical proof in the calculation 0.08 mm (thickness of paper) multiplied by 2 to the 43rd power, meaning the height grows exponentially. However, even a large sheet of newspaper can be folded only up to 7 times (try it if you don't believe it!). Therefore, we can say something theoretically possible is often practically impossible. After all, at present it is obviously more practical to rely on a rocket to get us to the moon.

As was discovered fairly recently, it is false to assume that the moon has no air. The fact that there is air contained in a very thin atmosphere was confirmed by NASA in the 1980's. However, the moon's air consists of sodium and potassium, and is 1/100 quadrillionth as thin as that of the earth, so it is almost equivalent to a true vacuum.

It also has long been believed that there was no water on the moon, but the existence of a large amount of ice around its south pole was confirmed by NASA in 2009.

　The moon has a large influence on the ebb and flow of the earth's oceans. This effect of the moon causes the earth to rotate slightly slower at a rate of one second every 100,000 years. Conversely speaking, in the past the moon was closer to the earth than now, and the earth's rotation was faster. For instance, 400 million years ago, one day was made up of 22 hours, with one year being 400 days. Surprisingly, soon after the formation of the earth, one year was 2000 days.

　In recent years there has been an interesting theory that the sediment of the moon can save mankind. On the moon's surface, there exists 1.03 million tons of soil containing helium 3. It is estimated that the nuclear fusion of helium 3 with heavy hydrogen will produce energy equivalent to the amount needed to sustain our fuel needs for 2,000 years on earth. This nuclear fusion gives off almost no radiation. Since oil is a finite resource and there are dangers in relying on nuclear energy, helium 3 is said to have the potential to greatly benefit the future of mankind.

NOTES

rocketry ロケット工学 / **astonishing** 驚くばかりの / **mathematical** 数学の / **multiply A by B** AにBを掛ける / **2 to the 43rd power** 2の43乗 / **grow exponentially** 指数関数的(ねずみ算的)に増加する / **theoretically** 論理的に / **practically** 実際には / **practical** 現実的な / **fairly recently** つい最近 / **sodium** ナトリウム / **potassium** カリウム / **quadrillionth** 1000兆番目の / **vacuum** 真空 / **south pole** 南極 / **NASA** (アメリカの)航空宇宙局 / **ebb and flow** （潮の）干満 / **rotate** 自転する / **slightly** わずかに / **conversely** 逆に / **formation** 形成 / **sediment** 土砂、沈殿物 / **helium 3** ヘリウム3 / **nuclear fusion** 核融合 / **heavy hydrogen** 重水素 / **give off** 放出する / **radiation** 放射線 / **a finite resource** 有限の資源

COMPREHENSION

次の英文が本文の内容と一致する場合はT、一致しない場合はFを記入しましょう。

1. (　) According to mathematics, folding a piece of paper 43 times should allow it to stack to a size that reaches the moon.
2. (　) The moon has breathable air but not water.
3. (　) The atmosphere on earth is 1/100 quadrillionth as thin as that of the moon.
4. (　) 400 million years ago, one year on earth contained 2000 days.
5. (　) The use of helium 3 can produce an energy source that is equivalent to the amount needed for 2000 years on earth.

Chapter 17 – *The Mystery of the Moon*

GRAMMAR

次の英文の空所に入れるのに正しい語句を (A) 〜 (D) から選びましょう。

1. TV programs that can be enjoyed by young and old (　　　) are rare at the moment.
    (A) alike　　　(B) either　　　(C) invariably　　　(D) respectively

2. Your digital camera is (　　　) better than mine. So, I felt like buying a new one.
    (A) pretty　　　(B) more　　　(C) much　　　(D) very

3. The professor has a tendency to teach us in an (　　　) technical way, so most of us do not fully understand what he says.
    (A) extraordinary　　(B) extraordinarily　　(C) entire　　(D) utmost

4. (　　　), Susan appeared at the party. I thought she would not come, because she is a very reserved person.
    (A) Astonish　　(B) Astonishing　　(C) Astonishingly　　(D) To astonish

5. My car engine gave (　　　) on the way to work the other day; therefore, I was not able to go to my office in time for the important meeting.
    (A) off　　　(B) in　　　(C) through　　　(D) out

<文法を理解する>　17. 副詞の位置

副詞は名詞以外であれば修飾することができます。そして、副詞の位置も比較的自由で、副詞は英文に比較的自由に入れることができます。しかし、比較的自由といっても、ルールがないわけではありません。以下が副詞を英文に入れる際の位置です。

　A , B 主語 C 動詞 X D , E .

(1) C の位置
　　always（いつも）のような頻度副詞（頻度を表す副詞）が置かれます。
(2) Dの位置
　　hard（一生懸命に）のような様態副詞（動詞を修飾する副詞）が置かれます。
(3) A / B / E の位置
　　surprisingly（驚くことに）のような文修飾の副詞（文を修飾する副詞）が置かれます。
注：Bにはyesterdayのような時を表わす副詞（文副詞に分類されない）が現れることが多い。
※Xは動詞に後続する要素（目的語や補語など）を表しています。

COMPOSITION

次の英文の（　　）内の単語を並べ換えて、意味の通る文にしましょう。

1. A lion's pride's survival (prowess / lionesses / depends / hunting / of / on / their / the); large male lions with great manes are poor at hunting because they are too heavy.
   (　　　　　　　　　　　　　　　　　　　　　　　　　　　　　　　　　　　　)

2. Pi is a number that goes on and on forever, (is / equivalent / twenty-two / but / to / sevenths / nearly / it).
   (　　　　　　　　　　　　　　　　　　　　　　　　　　　　　　　　　　　　)

3. Ultraviolet (on / negative / rays / a / health / humans' / have / influence), causing adverse effects such as wrinkles and spots on the skin, skin cancer, and cataracts, a type of eye disease.
   (　　　　　　　　　　　　　　　　　　　　　　　　　　　　　　　　　　　　)

4. Forests in the world (decrease / per / at / hectares / of / the / 521,000 / rate) hour, which means forests corresponding to 127 times the area of Tokyo Dome disappear each hour.
   (　　　　　　　　　　　　　　　　　　　　　　　　　　　　　　　　　　　　)

5. Solar power (the / the / solve / has / to / potential / generation / problem) of energy shortages in the future.
   (　　　　　　　　　　　　　　　　　　　　　　　　　　　　　　　　　　　　)

★英語表現の小箱１７★　文副詞 surprisingly について

　本文で surprisingly が出てきましたが、これは主観的な気持ちを表します。だから「驚いたことに」と訳されるわけです。様態副詞 (quickly や elegantly など) とは異なり、否定文の前にも来ます。しかし、客観的な文ではないので疑問文にできません。

　○ Surprisingly, John didn't eat anything.
　（＝驚いたことにジョンは何も食べなかった）
　× Quickly, John didn't eat anything.
　× Surprisingly, will the shy girl speak in public?
　○ Is it surprising that the shy girl will speak in public?
　（＝その内気な少女が人前で話すのは驚くべきことですか）

Chapter 17 – *The Mystery of the Moon*

🎧 LISTENING & DICTATION   CD 2-15

次の会話を聞いて、空所に単語を埋めましょう。

A: In recent years I've come to be intrigued by the moon. I first learned about the moon in (1.   ) in my astronomy class. I came away with the feeling that the moon is kind of mysterious. For example, since its (2.   ) cycle and rotation cycle are the same, the moon will always face the same way towards Earth. This is well known, though. There are other more interesting (3.   ) about the moon.

B: Can you give me some more examples? Like, it's made of (4.   )?

A: No, it's not, but the (5.   ) size of the moon and the sun seen from the earth are the same.

B: And that's why we have (6.   ) solar eclipses. That's common knowledge.

A: How about this? There are many large lunar craters on the reverse side of the moon. It's (7.   ) that the depth of each large crater is about six kilometers regardless of its size. You'd think that each crater should have a depth in proportion to the size of the meteorite or asteroid that impacted there. So, a larger crater should be deeper than a smaller one. But that's not the (8.   ). Weird, right?

B: Is that so? I never heard that.

A: Furthermore, the moon seems to be hollow. It is said that an artificial quake occurred for 55 minutes after the landing of Apollo 12's lunar module. This specifically points to the moon being (9.   ). The structure of the moon seems to be sufficient to cause even longer quakes. The relative density of the moon is much smaller than that of the earth, which is also (10.   ) that the moon is hollow.

B: Alright, alright! The moon has fascinated humans throughout history and will continue to do so far into the future, I get it. It's pretty easy to see why.

TIPS 科学よもやま話１７　月のクレーターはなぜ浅い？

　月の謎の１つにクレーターの深さがあります。大きさにかかわらず約６キロと一定だからです。例えば、直径1,300キロのマーレ・オリエンターレ・クレーターは、直径60キロの隕石［いんせき］が衝突したと考えられていますが、このように巨大な隕石が激突すれば、少なくとも100キロの深さのクレーターができると思われます。でも、クレーターはやはり約６キロ。これはなぜでしょうか。実は、月の地殻が氷で出来ていると考えると説明できるのです。隕石が激突し時きに深いクレーターは出来ますが、その時に発生した熱で氷が溶けて、クレーター内部を埋めるからです。そしてまた平坦な地形を形成します。月の表面は薄い岩石層で覆われているため、盛り上がった部分はそのまま残ります。

CHAPTER 18
Developments in Space Food

人は食事をしないと生きていくことはできません。それは宇宙でも同じです。しかし、地球とは異なり、宇宙での食事には食べ物自体にさまざまな制約があります。それはどのような制約でしょうか。また、どのような宇宙食が開発されているのでしょうか。

◀ VOCABULARY CHECK ▶

次の単語について、その定義を選び結びつけましょう。

1. withstand • • (A) to forcefully take in liquid, air, etc.
2. transport • • (B) to accept that something is true
3. suck • • (C) to formally forbid someone to do something
4. prohibit • • (D) to take something from one place to another
5. acknowledge • • (E) to be strong enough not to be hurt or damaged

PASSAGE

Space food refers to the specially prepared food that astronauts can eat in space. There are seven basic requirements of food for use in space.

It should have a long shelf life since food supplies cannot be flown in frequently. It should be light in weight since spacecrafts must adhere to strict
5 weight limits. It should not carry an odor since a spacecraft is a closed air space. It should not be something that can separate into small pieces as it may affect various devices. It should withstand temperature changes or physical shock since there is no knowing what will happen in a spacecraft. It should not need culinary preparation since there are no complex cooking facilities or time
10 to prepare the food on a spacecraft, and last but not least, it should be rich in nutrition since this is the only sustenance astronauts can have.

The cost of transporting the food is 8,800 dollars (about 890,000 yen) per kilogram; therefore, it is natural that in order to keep costs low, the food should be light weight and be able to be stored for long periods of time.

15 Fish is avoided due to its smell. Liquid foods are made sticky so they will not

Chapter 18 – *Developments in Space Food*

fly all over the insides of the craft, and soup is made to be sucked through a drinking straw.

An oven can be used, so food that can be boiled in a bag, can be. However, the use of a microwave oven is prohibited as it may adversely affect various devices on board the spacecraft.

During the age of the Apollo crafts, hot water began to be used and warm space food appeared. During the age of space shuttles, a wide variety of space food was invented including cans of French cuisine.

Twenty-eight items including ramen and curry have been acknowledged as Japanese space food. Natto, fermented soy beans that are rich in nutrition, was not approved, because it forms sticky threads. Surprisingly, the smell was considered to be within approved limits. Out of the 28 items, "Space Curry" and "Yohkan," or sweet bean jelly, are available to consumers. In a zero gravity environment, the sense of taste may change, so it is said that the food intentionally has a strong taste through additional spices and the like.

It is thought that astronauts will be able to eat any kind of food in the not-so-distant future.

NOTES

space food 宇宙食 / **astronaut** 宇宙飛行士 / **basic requirement** 基本的な要件 / **shelf life** 保存可能期間(＝賞味期限) / **odor** におい(イギリス英語ではodourと表記) / **culinary** 料理の / **cooking facility** 調理設備 / **nutrition** 栄養 / **sustenance** 食べ物 / **liquid food** 流動食 / **sticky** 粘着性の / **drinking straw** (飲み物の)ストロー / **microwave oven** 電子レンジ(microwaveでも可) / **adversely affect** 悪影響を与える / **cuisine** 料理 / **fermented** 発酵した / **soy bean** 大豆 / **sweet bean jelly** 羊羹［ようかん］/ **zero gravity** 無重力 / **intentionally** 意図的に / **and the like** など / **not-so-distant future** 遠くない将来

COMPREHENSION

次の英文が本文の内容と一致する場合はT、一致しない場合はFを記入しましょう。

1. (　) The weight of space food is not problematic.
2. (　) It is important for space food to be highly nutritious.
3. (　) In spacecrafts, microwave ovens are allowed.
4. (　) Ramen, curry and fermented soy beans are acknowledged as space food.
5. (　) The reason why space food has a strong taste is that in a zero gravity environment, the sense of taste may change.

GRAMMAR

次の英文の空所に入れるのに正しい語句を(A)～(D)から選びましょう。

1. You (　　　) as well come with us. I think you can learn a lot from the experience.

    (A) can　　　　(B) may　　　　(C) will　　　　(D) must

2. You will (　　　) speak English fairly well if you take this class for a minimum of six months.

    (A) can　　　　(B) be possible to　(C) ought　　　(D) be able to

3. Wendi has a gift for playing the violin, so her teachers recommended that she (　　　) abroad to enhance her ability.

    (A) goes　　　(B) shall go　　　(C) should go　　　(D) must go

4. That door (　　　) open. We need to fix it as soon as possible, or we won't be able to enter the bedroom.

    (A) will　　　　(B) will not　　　(C) have to　　　(D) don't have to

5. Before our final exam, our teacher said, "I (　　　) not emphasize this point enough." Thus, we were convinced that the point he was making would appear on the exam.

    (A) can　　　　(B) may　　　　(C) must　　　　(D) should

<文法を理解する> 18. 注意すべき助動詞

助動詞には、may / can / will / should / mustといった基本的な助動詞の他にも、注意すべきものとして、次のような助動詞があります。

　(1) ought to
shouldと同じで、義務(～すべき)と当然の推量(～のはずだ)の２つの用法があります。

　(2) used toとwould
used toとwouldはともに過去の習慣的動作(以前はよく～した)という用法があります。しかし、過去の状態(昔は～であった)という用法はused toにしかありません。また、used toは常に現在との対比が意識されますが、wouldにはそのような意識はありません。さらに、used toは肯定文・否定文・疑問文で使うことができますが、wouldは肯定文でしか使えないという点にも注意しましょう。

Chapter 18 – *Developments in Space Food*

COMPOSITION

次の英文の(　　　)内の単語を並べ換えて、意味の通る文にしましょう。

1. (in / to / current / question / project / while / the / referring), the researcher made some necessary observations on how to improve certain points.
   (　　　　　　　　　　　　　　　　　　　　　　　　　　　　　　　　)

2. Nancy temporarily (expert / are / when / to / adheres / divided / opinions / neutrality) about something, and gives much more consideration about it.
   (　　　　　　　　　　　　　　　　　　　　　　　　　　　　　　　　)

3. Any machine that can be made by humans is not perfect; (kind / problems / of / knowing / there / what / is / no) will occur over extended usage.
   (　　　　　　　　　　　　　　　　　　　　　　　　　　　　　　　　)

4. The oceanographer (vessel / board / for / probe / the / on / was / deep-sea) some time and sent a series of significant data to his research team.
   (　　　　　　　　　　　　　　　　　　　　　　　　　　　　　　　　)

5. There (in / is / species / an / of / extraordinarily / variety / wide) the world of insects; now over 800,000 species are known, accounting for over 50% of all living things.
   (　　　　　　　　　　　　　　　　　　　　　　　　　　　　　　　　)

★英語表現の小箱18★　　availableの語法

本文でavailableという単語が出てきますが、この単語の語法に注意をしましょう。

・利用できる，役に立つ，手元にある，入手可能な
  → Plenty of time is available.（時間はたっぷりある）
    The service is available to members only.
    （このサービスは会員だけが利用できる）
・（人が）手が空いている，（人が）…に出席可能である [for…]
  → Are you available for the meeting.（その会議に出席できますか）
・有効である，通用する
  → This card is available for two years.（このカードは2年間有効である）

LISTENING & DICTATION

CD 2-17

次の会話を聞いて、空所に単語を埋めましょう。

A: So did you find out (1.　　　) it takes to be an astronaut in Japan?

B: Yes, as promised, I did. The requirements for becoming an astronaut in Japan include having Japanese nationality and graduating from a university with a degree in a science-related discipline. You're a student at the Tokyo University of Science. In that (2.　　　), you'll have no problem so far.

A: I plan on graduating, so yeah.

B: An applicant should be (3.　　　) in scientific expertise with a background including scientific studies, (4.　　　) or development, ideally for more than three years.

A: I see. That requires commitment. It may not be a good idea for me to waste time working at a (5.　　　) company after graduation.

B: You should be healthy both physically and mentally. You must also be able to work well with others. Your height should be between 149 and 193 cm. Your (6.　　　) should be more than 0.1 without glasses, and more than 1.0 after (7.　　　). Last but not least, English proficiency is also important.

A: My height and vision are not problematic, but being (8.　　　) in English is going to take some time. I have to study hard for my English courses at school now. It's tough, but I'd like to be able to (9.　　　) the STEP first grade exam in the not-so-distant future.

B: Yes, English is a prerequisite for most international occupations. That's quite natural. Good luck. I'll be (10.　　　) for you.

TIPS 科学よもやま話18　宇宙食の面白話

　宇宙食を初めて食べた人は、1961年に旧ソ連の宇宙船「ボストーク2号」に搭乗したチトフという名前の宇宙飛行士です。

　宇宙食がおいしくないという不満から、1965年に勝手にターキーサンドイッチを持ち込んだ飛行士がいました。アメリカ人のジョン・ヤングでした。機器が汚れたり、食中毒などが起こる可能性があると指摘されましたが、これをきっかけに宇宙食の改善が進められました。

　さらに、宇宙ステーションなどでの長期滞在では、単調な生活となるので、食事は大きな気分転換となります。デザートなどを充実させることも重要な課題の１つであるといえます。地上でもデザートはうれしいものですが、宇宙ではストレス解消に大きく役立っているといえるのです。

CHAPTER 19

Pluto

かつては惑星と考えられていた冥王星ですが、現在は準惑星に分類されています。そもそも、冥王星とはどのような天体なのでしょうか。また、惑星、準惑星、小惑星とはそれぞれどのような基準で天体を区分したものなのでしょうか。

◀ VOCABULARY CHECK ▶

次の単語について、その定義を選び結びつけましょう。

1. memorize ・　　・ (A) to disappear suddenly
2. vanish ・　　・ (B) to move in a circle around a central point
3. question ・　　・ (C) to feel or express doubt about something
4. revolve ・　　・ (D) to intentionally retain knowledge of something
5. clear ・　　・ (E) to remove something from a place

PASSAGE

CD 2-18

　Do you know the Japanese phrase: Sui-Kin-Chi-Ka-Moku-Do-Ten-Kai-Mei? This is the easiest way for Japanese to memorize the planets of the solar system, or at least it was. However, in 2006 this mnemonic device became shorter when Mei was dropped.

　Originally, the phrase was an acronym made up of the first Chinese character of each planet in the solar system. The characters mean water, gold, earth, fire, wood, soil, heaven, sea, and Hades. These refer to Mercury, Venus, Earth, Mars, Jupiter, Saturn, Uranus, Neptune and Pluto respectively. The fact that "Mei" vanished does not mean Pluto itself disappeared from the solar system. The truth is that Pluto is now classified as a dwarf planet.

　Since its discovery in 1930, Pluto has always been regarded as an unusual planet compared to the others. This is mostly due to the fact that Pluto has a long, erratic elliptical orbit. It was also confirmed in 1978 that Pluto is one five hundredth the mass of Earth. In other words, its mass is far smaller than that of Earth. This is striking because its mass was considered to be about the same as Earth's or larger when it was discovered.

　For the foregoing reasons, scientists began to question the classification of Pluto as an actual planet. The present definitions of the three categories of astronomical bodies revolving around the sun are as follows:

Planet: A stellar object that revolves around the sun (No.1) with sufficient enough mass to make itself globular (No.2). It clears other heavenly bodies from its orbit (No.3).

Dwarf Planet: A stellar object sharing the same traits as No.1 and No.2 above. However, it does not clear other heavenly bodies from its orbit, and is not a satellite.

Small Solar System Bodies: This includes most of the astronomical bodies revolving around the sun with the exception of planets and dwarf planets. This category includes planetoids, comets and the like.

　Dwarf planets and planetoids are given minor-planet identification numbers by the MPC (Minor Planet Center). In the end, Pluto was classified as a minor planet and given the identification number 134340, which means it is the 134,340th minor planet ever discovered.

NOTES

planet 惑星 / **solar system** 太陽系 / **mnemonic device** 記憶法 / **originally** 元は / **acronym** 頭字語 / **Mercury** 水星 / **Venus** 金星 / **Mars** 火星 / **Jupiter** 木星 / **Saturn** 土星 / **Uranus** 天王星 / **Neptune** 海王星 / **Pluto** 冥王星 / **respectively** 順番に / **classify** 分類する / **dwarf planet** 準惑星 / **erratic** 風変わりな / **elliptical** 楕円の / **orbit** 軌道 / **one five hundredth** 500分の1 / **striking** 特筆すべき / **forgoing** 前述の / **definition** 定義 / **category** 区分 / **astronomical body** 天体(= heavenly body) / **stellar** 星の(← star) / **globular** 球体の(← globe) / **trait** 特徴 / **satellite** 衛星 / **small solar system body** 太陽系小天体(太陽系に存在する、惑星・準惑星より小さい天体のことで、小惑星や彗星[すいせい] などが該当) / **planetoid** 小惑星 / **comet** 彗星 / **identification number** 識別番号 / **MPC (Minor Planet Center)** 小惑星センター（小惑星と彗星の発見や軌道などに関する情報収集・提供を行う組織）/ **in the end** ついに

COMPREHENSION

次の英文が本文の内容と一致する場合はT、一致しない場合はFを記入しましょう。

1. (　) Pluto was discovered in 1930.
2. (　) The mass of Pluto is larger than that of the earth.
3. (　) One of the requirements to be a dwarf planet is that it be a satellite.
4. (　) Comets are classified under "small solar system bodies."
5. (　) The identification number of Pluto by MPC is 134340.

GRAMMAR

次の英文の空所に入れるのに正しい語句を (A) 〜 (D) から選びましょう。

1. The wealthy old man does not want his prodigal son to be (　　　) to his estate, for obvious reasons.

   (A) heiress　　(B) a heir　　(C) an heir　　(D) an heiress

2. I saw a very interesting novel at the bookstore yesterday. So, I bought (　　　) today.

   (A) book　　(B) a book　　(C) the book　　(D) ones

3. I know (　　　) importance of global communication, especially for better mutual understanding.

   (A) an　　(B) the　　(C) such　　(D) its

4. Everyone knows that (　　　) rises in the east and sets in the west but most people are not sure how the sun behaves in regard to other planets.

   (A) sun　　(B) suns　　(C) a sun　　(D) the sun

5. My daughter is not home but at (　　　) now. She will be home by six.

   (A) school　　(B) schools　　(C) a school　　(D) the school

＜文法を理解する＞　19. a teacher と the teacher の違い

次の2つの文について考えてみましょう。

(1) Tom is a teacher.　　(2) Tom is the teacher.

(1)と(2)の英文の違いは、teacher に対する冠詞が a か the かということだけです。英語では a / an は新情報を表し、the は旧情報を表すので、(1)では a teacher が新情報であるため Tom が旧情報になるのに対して、(2)では the teacher が旧情報であるため Tom が新情報となります。このことを和訳に反映させると以下のようになります。

(1) トムは(他の職業に就いているのではなく)教師です。

(2) (他の誰かではなく)トムが教師です。

日本語だけをみると、「は」と「が」の違いだけのように感じるかもしれませんが、伝えたいニュアンスは全く違います。英語では a と the が違うというだけでも大きな違いが生まれるので、冠詞についてもしっかりと学ぶようにしましょう。

✎ COMPOSITION

次の英文の(　　　)内の単語を並べ換えて、意味の通る文にしましょう。

1. Generally speaking, an (protons / is / up / made / and / of / nucleus / atomic) neutrons; however, a hydrogen nucleus consists of one proton and zero to two neutrons.
   (　　　　　　　　　　　　　　　　　　　　　　　　　　　　　　　　)

2. Some scientists say viruses are not organisms, and their (mostly / that / to / due / fact / is / idea / the) viruses are incapable of autonomous reproduction and growth.
   (　　　　　　　　　　　　　　　　　　　　　　　　　　　　　　　　)

3. The mass of Jupiter, the largest planet of the solar system, (than / of / the / is / that / sun / smaller / far); it is nearly equal to one thousandth of the mass of the sun.
   (　　　　　　　　　　　　　　　　　　　　　　　　　　　　　　　　)

4. When writing papers, you may be confused (you / all / old / from / data / unless / clear / the) your documents; what you need is a fresh slate to work with.
   (　　　　　　　　　　　　　　　　　　　　　　　　　　　　　　　　)

5. A bat is no more a bird than a whale is a fish; in short, not (whales / bats / classified / mammals / as / are / but / only).
   (　　　　　　　　　　　　　　　　　　　　　　　　　　　　　　　　)

★英語表現の小箱１９★　「構成」を表す表現

本文では(be) made up of ～（～で構成されている）という表現が出てきましたが、重要な同義表現が合計４つあります。

- １語で　　comprise ～
- ２語で　　consist of ～
- ３語で　　be composed of ～
- ４語で　　be made up of ～

注：be made of ～は「～で出来ている」という意味で、～の部分に材料が来ます。
　→ The desk is made of wood.（その机は木で出来ている）

LISTENING & DICTATION

CD 2-19

次の会話を聞いて、空所に単語を埋めましょう。

A: Which planet intrigues you the most?

B: I like Pluto because it's kind of (1.   ). Its orbit is erratic. Like me.

A: Sorry to say, but the (2.   ) is that Pluto is not a planet now. It was discovered in 1930 by Clyde Tombaugh, and at that time, it was considered a planet, but it was (3.   ) to the status of a dwarf planet in 2006 because it was found to be (4.   ) in the requirements of what it takes to be considered a planet.

B: That doesn't change anything It just makes me like it (5.   ), planet or not. I bet it's very cold there because it is so far from the sun. I like the cold.

A: "Cold" may be an understatement. It is said that the (6.   ) temperature of Pluto is minus 240 degrees Celsius. In physics, (7.   ) zero corresponds to minus 273 degrees Celsius, so it's nearly absolute zero; therefore, it's literally freezing.

B: Any idea what the (8.   ) of Pluto is?

A: Yes, it is about one 500th the mass (9.   ) Earth. A single revolution around the sun takes 248 years.

B: So I'd be dead before my first birthday if I (10.   ) born there. Does Pluto have satellites?

A: Yes, it's got five of them. You're crazy, you know that?

TIPS 科学よもやま話19　宇宙空間に水は豊富

　実は、宇宙空間には水が豊富に存在します。例えば、彗星は氷の塊で、土星のリングもほとんど氷で出来ています。土星の衛星であるミマス、テティス、ディオネ、レア、エンケラドゥスも全て氷で出来た衛星です。また、木星の衛星のエウロパ、ガニメデ、カリストの地殻も氷で出来ています。

　天王星も大気の下に厚さ1,600キロの氷の層があり、その下に超熱水が8,000キロの深さで存在するようです。海王星も、氷惑星であるとされています。

　太陽系でも指折りの極寒の星である冥王星も当然、表面は氷で出来ています。その氷は200キロの厚さで、その下に約100キロから170キロの厚さの海が存在する可能性があると、最近の研究で発表されました。

CHAPTER 20
Is the Earth an Iron Planet?

地球に対してどのようなイメージを持っていますか。多くの人は「青い星」や「水の惑星」と答えるかもしれません。しかし、実は、地球は「鉄の惑星」だったのです。それはどういうことでしょうか。

◀ VOCABULARY CHECK ▶

次の単語について、その定義を選び結びつけましょう。

1. element　・　・(A) a necessary part of something
2. oxide　　・　・(B) a colorless gas that is the lightest of all gases
3. planet　　・　・(C) a compound of oxygen and another chemical element
4. hydrogen ・　・(D) a large round object in space that moves around a star
5. ecology　・　・(E) the relation of living creatures to each other and to their environment

PASSAGE CD 2-20

　　Since it is covered in so much water, our blue planet, Earth, is classified as a water planet. This is because seas make up about 71% of the total surface of the earth. However, the total weight of water on earth is 0.02% of that of the earth. Moreover, 97.5% of the water is sea water, which without purification
5 and desalination cannot be used as drinking water or other practical uses.

　　Deep-sea submerged volcanoes contain significant amounts of iron, allowing unique organisms like the steal-clad shellfish known as the scaly-foot gastropod to exist. Its feet are covered in iron scales.

　　In fact, iron is the heaviest element in total of all the elements on earth. To
10 be more specific, the earth consists of oxides with iron, silicon and magnesium, with the iron in the earth accounting for 34.6% of the total weight of the earth. In short, about one third of its weight is that of iron. Therefore, the earth is actually an iron planet.

　　In the beginning of the universe, there was no iron; only hydrogen existed
15 and then helium. Gradually heavier elements came into being, and the universe

Chapter 20 – *Is the Earth an Iron Planet?*

developed with various elements combining or separating to form new elements. It is theorized that the universe will eventually converge into the most stable element, which is iron. At present the age of the universe is said to be 13.8 billion years old. An unknown billions of years beyond that, the universe may be entirely made up of iron.

The reason why everything will morph into an iron state remains a mystery; however, there is some significance in this. Since iron is easily available, cheap and easy to process, it is the most useful of metals for humankind. After the industrial revolution, the impact and utility of iron caused it to be referred to as the "Rice of Industry."

Since iron is a very important part of blood, it is indispensable to our health, but recently it has been discovered that it has a positive effect on the environment. Underneath Kansai Airport and Tokyo Bay's Umihotaru are support structures containing iron. These structures activated the sea's ecology nearby. Under its influence, seaweed is growing aplenty and fish populations are increasing. Iron will certainly continue to play a significant role in the life of humans as well as the universe. When considering that everything in existence will be iron a countless number of years from now, it is not hard to imagine why iron already plays such a significant part in our lives.

NOTES

classify A as B AをBに分類する / **make up ~ %** ~%を占める / **purification** 浄化 / **desalination** 脱塩 / **submerged volcano** 海底火山 / **significant** かなりの / **organism** 生物 / **steal-clad** 鋼鉄を纏[まと]った / **shellfish** 貝 / **scaly-foot gastropod** ウロコフネタマガイ / **scale** 鱗[うろこ] / **silicon** ケイ素 / **magnesium** マグネシウム / **helium** ヘリウム / **come into being** 出現する / **theorize** ~ ~という学説を立てる / **eventually** 最終的には / **stable** 安定した / **morph into ~** ~に変化する / **industrial revolution** 産業革命 / **impact** 反響 / **utility** 実用性 / **indispensable** 不可欠な / **positive effect** プラス効果 / **underneath** ~の下に / **support structure** 支持構造物 / **activate** 活性化する / **seaweed** 海藻 / **aplenty** 豊富に / **in existence** 存在する / **countless** 数えきれない / **play a significant part** 重要な役割を演じる

COMPREHENSION

次の英文が本文の内容と一致する場合はT、一致しない場合はFを記入しましょう。

1. (   ) Oceans and seas account for about 71% of the total surface of the earth.
2. (   ) Deep-sea submerged volcanoes are rich in iron.
3. (   ) Deep-sea submerged volcanoes consist solely of iron.
4. (   ) Two thirds of the total weight of the earth is made up of substances excluding iron.
5. (   ) At the birth of the universe, iron existed.

GRAMMAR

次の英文の空所に入れるのに正しい語句を(A) 〜 (D)から選びましょう。

1. You started to write that planning document three hours ago? I hope you (　　　) it.

    (A) already finish (B) have already finished
    (C) already have been finished (D) have finished already

2. (　　　) I do in the country, I am out of touch with the latest information.

    (A) Living as (B) As living (C) Lived as (D) As lived

3. Claire is (　　　) to work with because she is always coming in late when I meet her.

    (A) possible (B) impossible (C) possibly (D) impossibly

4. I think you can use a small plastic bottle as a flower pot, (　　　) cut off.

    (A) the top is (B) with its top (C) whose top (D) the top of which

5. Mr. Yamada has a lot of friends, (　　　) he went to university with.

    (A) many of them (B) many of which (C) many of that (D) many of whom

<文法を理解する>　20. 英語の曖昧性 II

次の英文について考えてみましょう。

　　John fought with Bill.

上記の英文を何と訳すでしょうか。確かに和訳は「ジョンはビルと戦いました」という意味になりますが、実は、この英文は2通りに解釈することができます。

(1) ビルが味方

　fightに対してwith句が修飾していると考える、つまりwith句が塊である場合、fight with ~ は「~と共同して戦う」という意味で、ジョンにとってビルは味方ということになります。ジョンとビルが組んでタッグマッチを行ったというふうに解釈することができます。

(2) ビルが敵

　fight withを1つの塊と考えると、文字通り「ビルと戦う」という意味なので、ジョンにとってビルは敵ということになり、ジョンは対戦相手のビルと戦ったという風に解釈することができます。こちらはイディオムとも解釈できるので、fight withが他動詞的に作用し、受動態にすることができます。

Chapter 20 – *Is the Earth an Iron Planet?*

COMPOSITION

次の英文の(　　)内の単語を並べ換えて、意味の通る文にしましょう。

1. An adult African elephant is considered the heaviest animal, (10 / the / about / total / is / weight / which / of) tons.
    (　　　　　　　　　　　　　　　　　　　　　　　　　　　)

2. (woods / butter / the / known / are / as / avocados / of), while another name of grapes is milk of the field.
    (　　　　　　　　　　　　　　　　　　　　　　　　　　　)

3. The number of penguins raised in Japan (the / fourth / of / for / number / total / accounts / one) of them in the world.
    (　　　　　　　　　　　　　　　　　　　　　　　　　　　)

4. The wings of even completely different species like insects (birds / to / into / shapes / tend / converge / similar / and).
    (　　　　　　　　　　　　　　　　　　　　　　　　　　　)

5. The eating of (our / effect / a / may / positive / have / on / bananas) health; bananas are said to help strengthen our immune system by increasing white blood cells.
    (　　　　　　　　　　　　　　　　　　　　　　　　　　　)

★英語表現の小箱２０★　主な元素を英語で言えますか？

本文ではhydrogen（水素）やhelium（ヘリウム）などが出てきましたが、「○素」で表記される日本語の元素名に当たる英語を示しておきましょう。

- 炭素⇒ carbon
- 水素⇒ hydrogen
- 酸素⇒ oxygen
- 窒素⇒ nitrogen
- 硼[ホウ]素⇒ boron
- 砒[ヒ]素⇒ arsenic
- 臭素⇒ bromine
- 弗[フツ]素⇒ fluorine
- 珪[ケイ]素⇒ silicon
- 塩素⇒ chlorine
- 沃[ヨウ]素⇒ iodine

LISTENING & DICTATION

次の会話を聞いて、空所に単語を埋めましょう。

A: How much do you know about the earth's mantle?

B: Not much. Only what I've heard. It's part of the (1.   ) inside the earth, right?

A: No, the mantle and magma are different. The mantle is a (2.   ) consisting of hard rocks, which lie from 30 to 2,900 kilometers below the surface. In contrast, magma (3.   ) to the melted rocks that lie in the crust or part of the mantle.

B: Learn something new every day, I suppose. Okay, so you say the mantle is a layer of rocks, which means it's (4.   ). The mantle alone can't be hot enough to melt stone, right?

A: You're correct, but the temperature of the mantle is between 1,500 degrees Celsius near the crust and 3,000 degrees Celsius on the (5.   ) of the earth's outer core.

B: What color is the mantle, then? We're talking about something buried deep in the earth. I'd guess it's black or maybe brown.

A: Interestingly, the mantle is hot enough to emit brilliant light, so if we could cut the earth in half, the mantle would actually be glowing brilliantly. This is called thermal (6.   ). If this radiating light was somehow turned off, you'd see magnificent jewel-encrusted rock everywhere. To be more specific, the upper mantle is pure green, and its middle part is dark green with a blue tinge, the deeper we go. Only the lower mantle from 660 kilometers below the surface seems to be dark brown.

B: Incredible! The upper mantle is full of (7.   )? I'm imagining a kind of (8.   ) realm; a world of purity, free from the pollution and troubles that (9.   ) us humans around.

A: The mantle is constantly moving, too. This movement is indispensable to Earth. Without this slow and (10.   ) movement, we could not enjoy such luxuries as hot springs.

TIPS 科学よもやま話20　人類は地球内部の99%を見ていない

　地下鉄が通る最深地点は地下42.3メートル、人間が到達した最深部は地下3.9キロ、掘った穴の最深記録は12キロ。地球は赤道の半径が約6,378キロだから、人類は地球内部の99.8%を知らないことになります。

　地殻の下の約2,800キロの厚さの部分がマントルで、超スローで対流しています。その速度は1年間で10cmセンチほど。カタツムリの50万分の1の速さです。

　地下2,900キロから2,000キロ続くのが、外核で、鉄が溶けた海が広がっています。その下にある地球中心部である内核は、温度よりも圧力が勝ち、鉄の塊となっています。ちょうど鉄の惑星が地球内部に入っているイメージです。

TEXT PRODUCTION STAFF

edited by 編集
Eiichi Kanno 菅野 英一
Kimio Sato 佐藤 公雄

English-language editing by 英文校閲
Bill Benfield ビル・ベンフィールド

cover design by 表紙デザイン
Lighthouse Co., Ltd. 株式会社ライトハウス

text design by 本文デザイン
Ruben Frosali ルーベン・フロサリ

CD PRODUCTION STAFF

narrated by 吹き込み者
Erika Wiseberg (AmE) エリカ・ワイズバーグ（アメリカ英語）
Chris Wells (AmE) クリス・ウェルズ（アメリカ英語）

Science Wisdom
科学から学ぶ知恵

2015年1月20日 初版 発行
2024年3月15日 第9刷 発行
著 者 石井 隆之 梶山 宗克
Joe Ciunci
発行者 佐野 英一郎
発行所 株式会社 成美堂
〒101-0052 東京都千代田区神田小川町3-22
TEL 03-3291-2261 FAX 03-3293-5490
https://www.seibido.co.jp

印刷・製本 倉敷印刷（株）

ISBN 978-4-7919-3382-2　　　　　　　　　　Printed in Japan

・落丁・乱丁本はお取り替えします。
・本書の無断複写は、著作権上の例外を除き著作権侵害となります。

MEMO

MEMO